All Lost in Wonder

"See, Lord, at thy service low lies here a heart
Lost, all lost in wonder at the God thou art."

*From Gerard Manley Hopkins' version
of St. Thomas Aquinas' ADORO TE.*

Sermons on Theology and Life

ALL LOST IN WONDER

by Walter J. Burghardt, S.J.

Professor of Patristic Theology, Woodstock College

The Newman Press · 1960 · Westminster, Maryland

Imprimi potest: JOHN M. DALEY, S.J.
Provincial, Maryland Province
January 15, 1960

Nibil obstat: EDWARD A. CERNY, S.S., S.T.D.
Censor Librorum

Imprimatur: ✠ *Imprimatur:* ✠ FRANCIS P. KEOUGH, D.D.
Archbishop of Baltimore

Baltimore, April 25, 1960

The *nibil obstat* and *imprimatur* are official declarations that a booklet or pamphlet is free of doctrinal and moral error. No implication is contained therein that those who have granted the *nibil obstat* and *imprimatur* agree with the opinions expressed.

 # Foreword

F<small>OR</small> <small>EIGHT</small> years and a half (from February, 1951 to June, 1959) it was my good fortune to present a half-hour religious program regularly (monthly at first, then twice each month) over Station WWIN in Baltimore. This program had a twin aim: to offer a radio audience superior productions in the religious music of the ages, and to present Catholic theological thought attractively. The sermons in question stressed dogma rather than morality, belief rather than conduct, thought rather than action. For the most part, they were ten to twelve minutes in length; every so often, either the nature of the subject—the Trinity, for example—or some other circumstance dictated a longer presentation.

On several occasions I have been urged to make some of these sermons available to a wider audience. Those who counseled publication insisted that, despite the brevity of these talks, in them the redemptive message and the redemptive activity of Christ have been captured in winning and compelling fashion, without losing their depth and richness. It is with a certain reluctance that I have consented; for a sermon is written to be preached, it supposes a specific speaker and a specific audience, and on the printed page even truth can look pale and bloodless.

In preparing the manuscript for publication, I have discovered—not surprisingly—that the sermons fall into a number of familiar categories: God and creation, sin and Incarnation, the life of Christ and the life of the Christian, the Eucharist and the passion, the resurrection and the resurrectional life, our Blessed Lady, the so-called theological virtues (faith, hope, love), and eschatology or "the last things." And so have I ordered them here.

It may come as a surprise that the "practical application" is little in evidence in the pages that follow. The slight is deliberate. Over almost two decades of preaching I have grown steadily more convinced that the traditional "application" is discouragingly impractical without proportionate motivation—and the proper motivation for genuinely Catholic living is discoverable only in authentically Catholic doctrine presented intelligibly and attractively. Conversely, given intelligible presentation of the doctrine, the intelligent Catholic is frequently capable of making the concrete application for himself, with a minimum of explicit exhortation. Given attractive presentation, he will want to do so.

In quoting Scripture I have used various English versions —Douay, Knox, Kleist & Lilly, the Chicago Bible, the Confraternity Edition—at times to recapture more faithfully the sense of the original, at times for felicity of expression.

One final word. It would be less than gracious for a preacher not to express warm gratitude to that Spirit without whose aid, as St. Paul noted, "no one can say 'Jesus is Lord' " (1 Cor 12:3).

WALTER J. BURGHARDT, S.J.

Acknowledgments

THE AUTHOR and The Newman Press wish to thank the following for permission to reproduce copyrighted material:

Apostleship of Prayer, New York, for "Discovery," by Sister Mary Ignatius, S.S.J., from the February, 1942, issue of *The Messenger of the Sacred Heart.*

The Bruce Publishing Company, Milwaukee, for quotations from the New Testament in the translation of James A. Kleist, S.J., and Joseph L. Lilly, C.M.

Catholic Biblical Quarterly, Washington, D.C., for "The Elements of Old Testament Poetry," by W. H. McClellan, S.J.

The Commonweal, New York, for "East German Refugees," by Bertrand Schneider, from the February 8, 1952, issue of that magazine.

Henry Holt & Company, New York, for *Cyrano de Bergerac*, by Edmond Rostand, translated by Brian Hooker.

The Macmillan Company, New York, for "I See His Blood upon the Rose," by Joseph Mary Plunkett, from *The World's Great Catholic Poetry*, edited by Thomas

Walsh; and for "After the Annunciation," by Eileen Duggan, from *Poems*.

The Oxford University Press, Inc., New York, for *Poems of Gerard Manley Hopkins*, edited by W. H. Gardner. Copyright 1948 by the Oxford University Press, Inc.

Random House, Inc., New York, for *Lazarus Laughed*, by Eugene O'Neill, from *The Plays of Eugene O'Neill*.

Sheed & Ward, Inc., New York, for *The Confessions of St. Augustine*, translated by F. J. Sheed; *Damien the Leper*, by John Farrow; *The Water and the Fire*, by Gerald Vann, O.P.; and for quotations from the New Testament in the translation of Monsignor Ronald Knox.

Time, New York, for "Some Question," and "Those Who Lie in Jail," from the October 25, 1948 and the April 30, 1951 issues of that magazine. Copyright Time, Inc., 1948 and 1951.

The University of Chicago Press, Chicago, for quotations from *The Complete Bible: An American Translation*, edited by J. M. Powis Smith and E. J. Goodspeed.

The Viking Press, New York, for "The Creation," from *God's Trombones*, by James Weldon Johnson.

A. Watkins, Inc., New York, for *Creed or Chaos?*, by Dorothy L. Sayers, and published by Harcourt, Brace & Company, New York.

Sermons

God and Creation

1. The Trinity: Mystery of Love[1]

IN THE LIFE of a Christian—in your life and mine—there are two decisive moments. The first decisive moment is a beginning—the ageless words spoken over you as you opened your eyes on life: "I baptize you in the name of the Father, and of the Son, and of the Holy Spirit." The second decisive moment is an ending—the touching prayer the Church whispers to God as the Christian closes his eyes on life: "He has sinned, it is true, but at least he has not denied his belief in the Father, the Son, and the Holy Spirit." And in-between these moments lies a lifetime, a succession of moments dominated by a simple gesture, a ceaseless sign of the cross: "In the name of the Father, and of the Son, and of the Holy Spirit. Amen."

My dear friends: Christian life is lived in the shadow of a Trinity. And this "tremendous trifle" reminds us of a fact; the fact suggests a problem; and the problem begs for a solution. A fact—a problem—a solution.

The fact is simply told. God became man to do something and to say something. He became man to do something: to re-establish on a hill the oneness between God and man that

1 For the central idea of this sermon, and for some aspects in its development, I am indebted to a splendid chapter on the Trinity in Gaston Salet, S.J., *Richesses du dogme chrétien* (Le Puy: Editions Xavier Mappus, 1945), pp. 139-67.

had been ruptured in a garden—to recapture man's heart by a crucifixion. And He became man to say something: to tell us secrets unsuspected about God and about the mirror of God that is man—to recapture man's mind by a revelation.

What God *did* is a living proof that God loves men. The crucifixion echoes the tender syllables murmured by God to Israel in exile: "Can a woman forget her infant, so as not to have pity on the son of her womb? And if she should forget, yet will not I forget thee" (Is 49:15). The crucifixion etches in flesh—in Christ's flesh—an ecstatic truth: God is a Father —*my* Father.

But what God *said* is no less a lesson in love. God did not have to tell us His deepest secret, the life He lives alone without ever being lonely. He did not have to tell us just who and what He is; we could have been saved without it. And yet He did tell us in breathless accents the truths that come so coldly from human lips: "There is but one God. . . . In this one God there are three Persons: Father, Son, and Holy Spirit. . . . These three Persons are really distinct: the Father is not the Son, the Son is not the Father, the Holy Spirit is neither the Father nor the Son. . . . Each of these Persons is really and truly God. . . . And still there is but one God."

You see, God is not quite satisfied with being served; He wants to be known—and that is a precious proof of love. In fact, what God said has moved a Catholic layman to write boldly: "The revelation of the Trinity was in one sense a more certain proof even than Calvary that God loves men." For God's revelation etches in human minds—in your mind and mine—an ecstatic truth: God is a Father—the Father of *Christ.*

That is the fact: God has spoken, and His words are woven of love. But the problem remains: why *this* mystery? Why must I keep repeating "I believe in one God: Father,

Son, and Holy Spirit," when I can hardly express it without seeming to say something as silly as a square circle? Oh, I recognize, with Péguy, that "Jesus did not come down here to tell us trifles." I admit that, if God took the trouble to talk, He could hardly do better than to talk about Himself. I know that St. Paul was haunted by the Trinity, so much so that he could scarcely speak of Christ without bringing in Father and Holy Spirit. I know that for this truth the Church, a sorrowing mother, has watched thousands turn from her in hate; that on this issue the Christian world was rent, men were excommunicated and exiled, men died.

The Trinity, therefore, is a truth worth *dying* for. But the problem remains: is it worth *living* for? The stumbling block is not so much that my mind is bent low before mystery—that is a problem only for the proud. The anguish is far more acute: of what value is this mystery for contemporary living, for the Christian whose day is compounded of "sweat and blood and tears"? "From the dogma of the Trinity," a philosopher has insisted, "absolutely nothing can be drawn for practical life."

Is there a solution? One way of lending meaning to the mystery is to steal St. John's definition of God: "God is Love." On that score Augustine was stubborn: "You want to think of God [he said]. Why do you let your thoughts, your thinking, ramble here and there? God is nothing you imagine, nothing you think you understand. Do you want some foretaste of what God is? God is Love." And that is the point I shall make this afternoon: in the Trinity we find the perfect realization of perfect love; in God's secret life we glimpse the model-without-beginning for every love that has ever begun.

You see, love between persons makes a double demand. It demands that lover and beloved remain *two*, and it demands that the two be somehow *one*. In the first place, love between persons demands distinct persons. Love is "we"—a "you" and an "I." Whether I love God or another human being, I never cease to be myself. Teresa of Avila, caught up in God, never ceased to be Teresa, never became God. And the very human love of man and woman will always have something in it of the tragic love of Shakespeare's Othello and Desdemona, who fell "in love with what she fear'd to look on." Othello remains always the Moor, and Desdemona the Venetian. He a soldier, with his "dearest action in the tented field"; she "a maiden never bold, of spirit so still and quiet that her motion blush'd at herself."[2]

Yes, love demands "I" and "thou." But love forbids "mine" and "thine." What Augustine calls "those ice-cold words." The two, remaining two, must somehow be one. But man has long since learned a bitter-sweet lesson: oneness with an object beloved can be achieved only in terms of self-giving. To love is to give—to give of one's self. To love perfectly is to give until there is nothing left to give. It is only then that the two, remaining two, become perfectly one.

The marvelous thing about the Trinity is that it is the total realization of perfect love. God's secret is this: there is "I and thou" without "mine and thine." There is "I and thou": there are three Persons. The Father is not the Son; the Son is not the Father; the Holy Spirit is neither the Father nor the Son. Each is a real Person. But, strangely, there is no "mine and thine," no egoism. That one tremendous thing which makes God God—we call it the divine nature—that one tremendous thing which makes God God, the Father has it completely, the Son has it completely, the Holy Spirit has it completely. Very simply: no one has anything which the other does not have. Take three men—three men thinking and loving. Each man thinks with a different intellect, each man

2 William Shakespeare, *Othello, the Moor of Venice*, Act 1, Scene 3.

loves with a different will. Not so in God: Father, Son, and Holy Spirit know with one and the same intellect, love with one and the same will.

A mystery, of course—but the truth to cling to is this: in the Trinity there is neither "mine" nor "thine." The Father gives to the Son literally all that He Himself has—all that makes Him God—all that makes Him Love. And the Son, who receives from the Father literally all that He has, is a perfect Son, because He is the perfect image of His Father. The incredible thing is that the love with which the Son loves the Father is the selfsame infinite love with which the Father loves the Son. And this love of Father and Son, this love *is* the Holy Spirit.

My dear friends: One word sums up Christianity, and that word is love. And the Trinity is the model-without-beginning for every love that has ever begun. It is the model for our return of love *to God*. In the face of His love is it difficult to see that service of God, religion, is not slavery but a profound personal love? God and I are two; we must somehow be one. How? Listen to Augustine: "Are you looking for something to give to God? Give Him yourself."

In the Trinity we find above all what ought to be our *love for others*. You remember the powerful prayer of Christ for men: "I pray . . . that they all may be one, as thou, Father, in me, and I in thee" (Jn 17:20–21). Like the divine Persons, each of whom remains fully Himself, without the Father becoming the Son or the Son becoming the Father, so we too have to be utterly and splendidly ourselves, develop ourselves with all the wealth God has given us; it is the only way we have of being useful to others, by bringing to them, in a gift of ourselves, what we alone can give them. "The musical note helps the harmony only by being itself." Love demands "I and thou"; it forbids "mine and thine."

Of such love the Trinity is not merely the model; of such love the Trinity is the source. To love *like* God, we must love *through* God. The grace that we need is the grace that we have: Father, Son, and Holy Spirit *in* us, searing our souls. It is in them that you and I, remaining two, will become one.

2. Fatherhood: Human and Divine

IN THE LIFE of our Lord there is a touching scene. The apostles, rugged workingmen, approached Him one day, and with their hearts in their eyes they asked Him: "Lord, teach us to pray." And with all the keenness of His divine intellect and all the warmth of His human heart He answered: "When you pray, pray like this: 'Our Father, who art in heaven . . .'" (Mt 6:9; Lk 11:1-2). Our Father. . . .

You see, Christ our Lord told us a great deal about God. He told us that God is Life, that God is Love, that God is Goodness. But perhaps the most thrilling truth Christ our Lord trumpeted to the world, the secret not fully unlocked till Bethlehem, is the stirring truth: God is a Father.

St. Paul took up the same theme—God is a Father—but St. Paul added a profound clause: "I fall on my knees," he said, "to the Father of our Lord Jesus Christ, that Father from whom all fatherhood in heaven and on earth takes its title" (Eph 3:14–15). In other words, all fatherhood imaginable in creation is such and can be called such only because it is somehow a share in the Fatherhood of God. Every father on earth is a reflection of a Father in heaven.

And that is what I should like to burn into your souls today: that in your fatherhood each of you fathers is a little like God. To make that clear, I have to do three things: I have to (1) take you up to heaven, (2) wing you over to paradise, and (3) bring you down to earth again.

Fatherhood first flowered in heaven. Better still, fatherhood never had a beginning, because it always was. For God is a Father. God was always a Father. A perfect Father, because He gave to His only Son all that He Himself is, and kept back only what He could not give: His own Fatherhood. And His Son is a perfect Son, because He is the exact image, the perfect likeness, of His Father. That is why Christ our Lord, the Son of God, could say so simply: "I and the Father are one" (Jn 10:30).

That is fatherhood in heaven. But fatherhood is restless, even in heaven. And so, one day God took the dust of the earth; from that dust He built a body; that body He quickened with the breath of life, filled it with the Holy Spirit of Love. And the first human being looked upon his Father.

"Then the Lord God cast a deep sleep upon Adam" (Gn 2:21). And, while Adam slept, God took his flesh. From that flesh He built a body—the body of a woman—a woman vibrant with human life, a woman aglow with divine love. This first of women God brought to the first of men; Eve He gave to Adam, Adam to Eve, with His blessing.

That was, if I may speak humanly, one of the happiest moments in God's life. Clouds were sailing the sky, little buds were lifting their heads, the birds of the air and the beasts of the field dotted Eden's garden; but when the first man and the first woman looked up and knew their Father and loved Him, the rest of the world seemed awfully small.

There, in the garden of Eden, you have God again the perfect Father. Perfect, because He lavished on His children not only life but love; because He gave them not merely a garden of delights, but the gladness of grace, a share in His own divine life, a gift that made of Adam His son, and of Eve

His daughter. A gift that made Adam a lovable son and Eve a lovely daughter, simply because they were such striking images, such breathtaking reflections of their Father.

That was fatherhood in paradise. Now God could have remained forever satisfied with His own Fatherhood. He could have continued to fashion each human being entirely, body and soul. He could have filled the four corners of the earth, He could have brought you and me into existence, by simply repeating the act whereby He lifted Adam from the dust, and Eve from Adam. He could have created each human soul without waiting on anyone.

But this God did not choose to do. With a thoughtfulness divine, He chose instead to give human beings a share in His own tremendous power of creating, His own sublime prerogative of calling something out of nothing, His own divine right to give life. He chose to step back and wait until His creatures, a man and a woman, had played their part, before He would step in and, silently, without a sound or a gesture to betray His presence, complete the work of His human instruments with a human soul.

That is fatherhood on earth: a human reflection of fatherhood in heaven, a human echo of fatherhood in paradise. For, in your fatherhood, each father is a little like God. More like God, the more perfectly you image that fatherhood above, the more you give not merely of life but of love.

You will mirror God the Father if you mirror His *providence:* God's watchful care for His children. Do you remember the consoling words of Christ in the Sermon on the Mount? "I say to you, then, do not fret over your life, how to support it with food and drink, over your body, how to keep it clothed. . . . See how the birds of the air never sow, or reap, or gather grain into barns, and yet your heavenly Father feeds them. . . . And why should you be anxious over clothing? See how the lilies of the field grow; they do not toil or spin; and yet I tell you that even Solomon in all his glory was not arrayed like one of these. . . . Do not fret, then, asking, 'What are we to eat?' or 'What are we to drink?' or 'How shall we find clothing?' . . . You have a Father in heaven who knows that you need them all. Make it your first care to find the kingdom of God and His approval, and all these things shall be yours without the asking" (Mt 6:25–33). It's a striking thought, isn't it? Each father on earth, in giving to his children this day their daily bread, is imaging our Father in heaven. As "His eye is on the sparrow," so your love broods over the child of your shaping.

You will mirror God the Father if you mirror His *strength*: a gracious marriage of severity and liberality. Those whom He loves, God the Father chastises, yes; but He likewise leaves them room to grow to the full measure of Christian manhood. He respects the freedom of His children. Each human father, like St. Joseph, must sometimes seek his own little Christ in sorrow; and still he will leave him room to grow, as the first Christ grew, "in wisdom with the years, and in favor with God and with men" (Lk 2:52).

In short, you will mirror God the Father if, as Christ our Lord insisted, you are "perfect as your heavenly Father is perfect" (Mt 5:48). You know, a youngster takes tremendous pride in being a perfect image of his father. But that very fact puts a breathtaking burden on a father. If your child reflects you perfectly, will he be perfect? To be a perfect image of our Father-in-heaven is a tribute. To be a perfect image of our fathers-on-earth is a tribute only if our fathers are themselves images of God the Father.

It is a thrilling and a terrifying task, this task of playing God to your little ones, of lavishing life and love on human beings who are so obviously a mixture of the animal and the angel. The gifts you need for that task, gifts of nature and of grace, are so precious and so rare. You have one basic consolation, the words of our Lord: "you have a Father in heaven who knows that you need them all" (Mt 6:32).

3. The Heavens Are Telling

A POWERFUL poem on creation[1] opens with a moving scene:

> "And God stepped out on space,
> And He looked around and said:
> *I'm lonely—*
> *I'll make me a world."*

"I'm lonely." The idea is attractive, but not quite true. God was never lonely. There will never be more life, and there will never be more love, than the life of love lived by Father, Son, and Holy Spirit before the first puffs of cloud pirouetted in the sky. God could pine for nothing, simply because He had everything. God could never be lonely, because He was never alone.

And yet, God did make Him a world. Perhaps it *is* pure poetry to say, as James Weldon Johnson does, that "God smiled, and the light broke." It *is* fanciful to rhapsodize:

> "God rolled the light around in His hands
> Until He made the sun . . .
> And the light that was left from making the sun
> God gathered it up in a shining ball
> And flung it against the darkness,
> Spangling the night with the moon and stars."

1 "The Creation," in James Weldon Johnson, *God's Trombones* (New York: Viking Press, 1927), pp. 17–20.

It takes imagination to think that

> "God walked, and where He trod
> His footsteps hollowed the valleys out
> And bulged the mountains up . . ."

that

> "God spat out the seven seas—
> He batted His eyes, and the lightnings flashed—
> He clapped His hands, and the thunders rolled. . . ."

It *is* poetic to see God smile again, "and the rainbow appeared, and curled itself around His shoulder."

That is poetry. But, like all great poetry, so this too enshrines a tremendous insight. In tracing the world's beginning back to God's smile, the poet reveals two great truths: this material universe—this earth and sea and sky—all this was born of *God*, and all this was born of *nothing*.

All this was born of *God*. Earth, sea, and sky, as we know them, are the fruits of a glorious adventure. Each flower, each cloud, each mountain range goes back in time to some nameless, perhaps shapeless, certainly mysterious matter that is significant for an unforgettable reason: it was shaped by God. The opening lines of God's own book are unmistakable: "In the beginning, God created heaven and earth." It was God who smiled.

And all this was born of *nothing*. That first bit of matter, that small strange beginning of a world, is significant for another reason: before the world came into being, there was nothing for the eye to see, nothing for the ear to hear, nothing for the hand to fondle. God started with nothing, and He ended with something. "Let there be light," God commanded. "And there was light" (Gn 1:3). "He spoke," says the Psalmist, "and it was made" (Ps 32:9). That is God's "smile."

But *why* this divine smile? Why did God sow the seeds of hills and chaliced petals and rainbows? I said He was not lonely. I mean: He was not lonely as we are lonely. Human loneliness is a confession of poverty: there is something we want and cannot have. A little girl without her doll; Mary without her Christ; Adam outside paradise without his God. Human loneliness is a confession of poverty; God's loneliness was a profession of riches. He could not "get" anything, because He had everything. Beauty, love, power—why, God *is* Beauty, God *is* Love, God *is* Power. He could not get anything; but He could give something. And there is the secret behind creation, the key that lends meaning to mystery. God could give. . . .

You see, God realized that what He is could never be repeated: there cannot be two Gods. But God realized just as vividly that what He is could be faintly recaptured. Take an example. The Christ Jerusalem knew—the hungry, weary, sorrow-laden Christ—men will never see again. And yet clay can recapture His likeness, and saints will ever mirror His weariness and His hunger, the compassion of Christ and the Christ of the passion. In somewhat the same way, God saw that the visible could image the Invisible, that a whirlwind could reflect His power, a mountain mirror His majesty, surging waves His irrestistibleness, a star-flecked sky His breathtaking loveliness. God saw that He could *give*—oh, not just atoms and molecules, not sheer solids and liquids and gases; God saw that He could give of Himself. God saw that His own perfection could be imprisoned in something imperfect.

And so, when God gave this earth its beginning, He was but painting His own features on the canvas of a world. And there the God of power was powerless. He could fashion anything He pleased: ocean or rivulet, rain or rainbow. Yet He could fashion nothing unless it mirrored some perfection of

His. There is no peony that does not speak to us of Him. And if we miss its message, it is not because we know so little of the peony; it is rather that we know so little of God. Ignatius caught up in ecstasy as he eyed the sky at night, Teresa ravished by a rose, were not simply captivated by material things. They *were* captivated by sky and rose, but not sheerly that; they had caught for a shattering instant a glimpse of what God must be like. Their ecstasy but echoes the song of the Psalmist:

"See how the skies proclaim God's glory,
How the vault of heaven betrays His craftsmanship!

"Each day echoes its secret to the next,
Each night passes on to the next its revelation of
knowledge.

"No word, no accent of theirs
That does not make itself heard,

"Till their utterance fills every land,
Till their message reaches the ends of the earth."

(Ps 18:2–5)

Each blade of grass is God's struggle to paint His own portrait. And in each slender blade God succeeds and God fails. Each blade is something of God—therein lies its glory. And still God's face is hid. That is why God multiplied His face. That is why, with bold strokes and with subtle, He hurled star-worlds into space and streaked the rocks with veins of gold. Scripture tells us that of each individual day of creation God concluded: "It is good" (Gn 1:4, 10, 12, 18, 21, 25). Only of the whole work of His hands did He say: "It is *very* good" (Gn 1:31).

Dear friends in Christ: If there is any one fact of daily experience that is uniquely impressive, it is the eloquence of

God's creation. It is the selfsame truth that was trumpeted by St. Paul when he said of the heathen: "The knowledge of God is clear to their minds; God Himself has made it clear to them; from the foundations of the world men have caught sight of His invisible nature, His eternal power and His divineness, as they are known through His creatures" (Rom 1:19–20). From the lilies of the field we can learn about God. In looking on a lily we look through a mirror on God. But the converse is just as true: the more we know of God, the more we will know of the lily. It is only when the veil is lifted and we see our God face to face—only then will we see how much of Himself the Creator has put in His creatures—only then will we hear with naked ear what the heavens are trying to tell us.

4. Man: God's Image on Earth

In October, 1948, *Time* Magazine reported, without comment, the following news item: "Meeting in Paris last week to draft a Declaration on Human Rights, members of the U.N. Social, Humanitarian & Cultural Committee decided that it would be best to leave God out of Article I. After objections from the U.S.S.R. (as well as from Britain, China and India), Brazil withdrew its proposal to include the statement that 'all human beings were created in the image and likeness of God.' This proposition, said the Russian delegate, 'is much disputed' in the Soviet Union."[1]

My dear friends: Last month we watched God shape a world. We saw Him sow the seeds of hills and chaliced petals and rainbows. Not because He was lonely: God could never be lonely, because He was never alone. Not to "get" something: God could not get anything, because He had everything. But God could give—could give of Himself. He saw vividly that what He is could be faintly recaptured, that His own perfection could be imprisoned in something imperfect.

And yet, at this point God was still dissatisfied. Why? Why was He not satisfied to shape a stone? A stone, after all, is strangely like God, because like God it is *something*. Why was He not satisfied to fashion one fragile rose? Even

[1] *Time,* Oct. 25, 1948, p. 100.

more than a stone, a rose resembles its God, because like God it trembles with life—it is *alive*. Why could not the Creator have been content with a panther? Even more than a rose, a panther is patterned after God. Like God, it has a special kind of life; unlike the rose, it is *aware* of things. Above all, why could not God have rested as the artisan of angels? An angel is so very much like God, because like God it has a mind to *know*, and a will to *love*. An angel can mirror its Maker and know it; an angel can know its Lord and love Him.

But the fact is, God was not satisfied; He was not content with a stone or a rose or a panther, not even with an angel. You see, God's creation was aimed at a center: He had in mind a creature who would sum up in himself all creatures. Like the stone, he would be something. Like the rose, he would be a living thing. Like the panther, he would see and hear and touch and taste and smell. He would know and love with the angels. Each of these, in its own limited field, might well be superior to him. A stone might crush him; a rose would be far more fragrant; a panther could outrace him and an angel outthink him. But this creature alone would be a combination of them all, a fascinating blend of the animal and the angel, a world in miniature. For him the earth was fashioned; around him a universe would turn. This is the creature, wonderfully and fearfully made, on whom the curtain falls at the close of Scripture's first act:

"And God created man to His own image; to the image of God He created him; male and female He created them. And God blessed them, saying: 'Increase and multiply, and fill the earth, and subdue it, and rule over the fishes of the sea, and the fowls of the air, and all living creatures that move upon the earth' " (Gn 1:27–28). Little wonder that the Psalmist cried out in amazement:

"When I see thy heavens, the work of thy fingers,
The moon and the stars which thou hast formed;
What is man that thou shouldst think of him,
And the son of man that thou shouldst care for him?

"Yet thou hast made him but little lower than God,
And dost crown him with glory and honor!
Thou makest him ruler over the works of thy hands,
Thou hast put all things under his feet."

(Ps 8:3–6)

"Thou hast made him but little lower than *God*." However much men and nations may dispute it, we have God's word for it: man, every man, is "but little lower than God," simply because man, every man, is made by God to His image. Every human being bears a striking likeness to his Lord.

What does this mean? It means that, no matter who you are, no matter what your blood or skin or accent, male or female, you come into this world sharing two of God's precious perfections: you have the power to know, and you have the power to love.

As a human being, you have the power to know. Not as a plant knows where the sun is; that is a figure of speech. Not as a dog knows where an enemy lurks; that is a question of seeing and hearing and touching and tasting and smelling. Of earth's creatures, you alone can think. You alone can put 2 and 2 together and get 4. You alone can fashion the formula for an H-bomb. Only you can appreciate a sonata, a cantata, or a fugue. Only you can know God; of you alone could St. Paul insist: "From the foundations of the world *men* have caught sight of God's invisible nature, His eternal power and His divineness, as they are known through His creatures" (Rom 1:20).

As a human being, you have the power to love. Not as a

[23]

plant is drawn to the sun; not as one brute beast is attracted
to another. Your love is different from that on at least three
counts. In the first place, your love is not blind; it is a wide-
eyed thing that blossoms from knowledge, that flows from
your appreciation of what is good. Secondly, your love is not
simply a matter of getting, but of giving; and perfect love is
to give until there is nothing left to give—to lay down life
itself for the object of your love. And lastly, your love is free:
you can give it or you can withhold it, as you will. Wide-
eyed, selfless, and free: that is how human love images the
divine; that is how human love mirrors the love of God's only
Son, who, knowing full well the tragedy of His love, gave His
life gladly for the creatures He had shaped in His image.

But, in the Christian scheme of things, a human being is
made to image his God on a much loftier level. You are
destined, through that superlative gift we call grace, through
the indwelling of heaven within you, to image God in that
you are a son of God, or a daughter of God, after the pattern
of Him who is the one natural Son of God. Remember what
the early Christian writers kept thundering: "God became man
to make men gods." That higher resemblance reveals itself on
at least two levels—levels of knowledge and love.

Each of you is destined for the unique knowledge that is
vision: one day, as St. John promised, you "shall see God as
He is" (1 Jn 3:2). The eternal day will dawn when you shall
know God as God knows Himself; or, as St. Paul has it, you
shall see Him "face to face" (1 Cor 13:12). Now you see as
in a glass, darkly. Now you walk by faith; but even the
clouded vision that is faith is a share in God's knowledge of
Himself. The clearer and deeper your knowledge of God, the
more closely you resemble Him who knows Himself to perfection.

And in the state that is called grace, you own a gift that

is called charity: you love God somewhat as He loves Himself
—a love that will be perfected hereafter, but still a love that
has its beginning here. The more selflessly you love God for
what He is in Himself, the more closely will your love approximate the love of a Father who is a perfect Father, because He gives to His Son all that He Himself is, save the one
thing He cannot give—His Fatherhood; and the more closely
will your love approximate the love of a Son who is a perfect
Son, because He is the exact image of His Father.

And there, I submit, lies your dignity as human beings.
There, too, rests your equality, the equality of all men before
God. It is not so much that your flesh, like all human flesh,
was first fashioned from the dust of the earth; it is rather that
your soul, like every human soul, has been carved in the image
of God. You are so godlike, each one of you. You have been
created with a mind to know, a will to love; and you have
been redeemed so as to know God as God knows Himself, to
love God as God loves Himself.

That is why, fifteen hundreds years ago, St. Cyril of Alexandria could say with such conviction: "Of all the living
creatures on earth, there simply is none like man. For we were
not merely formed by God, as by a potter, from the dust of
the earth. We have been made to His image and likeness; we
have been enriched with the impress of His glory, gleaming
in our souls, even if we are, according to the flesh, earth and
of earth. Man, then," he concludes, "is an admirable, not a
contemptible creature: he is a little less than the angels."[2]

---

[2] Cyril of Alexandria, *Commentary on Isaias* 4, 2 (*Patrologia graeca* 70, 960).

5. Let Us Make Him a Help

WHEN GOD made Adam, He gave him a birthday gift. He gave him a garden of delights to dress and to keep; He gave him the beasts of the field for his pets, and the birds of the air for his song. He gave him God: God in his heart, and God to walk with him in the cool of evening.

But still God was not satisfied. Still there was an emptiness in the heart of Adam which all the flowers of paradise, all the animals in God's creation, even God Himself could not quite fill. And God put His finger on it when He said: "It is not good for man to be alone" (Gn 2:18).

"Then," Scripture tells us, "then the Lord God cast a deep sleep upon Adam" (Gn 2:21). And, while Adam slept, God took his flesh. Like a sculptor, He fashioned from that flesh a human body. Being God, He breathed into it the breath of life. And, when Adam woke, and rubbed his eyes, and looked, Adam smiled. Coming towards him was God—and God was leading by the hand the fairest thing in His creation: the first woman. Then Adam, in sheer ecstasy, touched by the Spirit of God, cried out: "This now is bone of my bone, and flesh of my flesh . . ." (Gn 2:23).

A lovely scene, this fashioning of Eve—but to what purpose? Had God simply said, "It is not good for man to be alone," we might have wondered. But God added something;

[27]

God said: "Let us make him a help like to himself" (Gn 2:18). A help. . . . In that tiny word, in that slender syllable, is mirrored the ideal of womanhood. For it implies, of its very nature, a giving. Not purely an ideal, but an ideal whose germ is within you; for, at the dawn of creation, God's gift to woman was the gift of giving.

In the ordinary designs of God's providence, a woman's first giving is to give herself—to another. But the gift can be given in any of three ways.

For most, that "other" is a single human being. And, as you kneel beside him, hand in hand, at an altar, as you link your lives for life, you give again. As minister of a sacrament —the sacrament of matrimony—you give to him the wedding gift of grace: God to dwell in his soul. A striking thought, isn't it? That in one sweeping, irrevocable gift you can give to another the two that are most dear to you: you can give yourself, and you can give God. It is a giving that grows with the years—a giving that gives rise to "such sweet sorrow," when you give, to earth and heaven too, other Christs—images of Christ born of your body—born rather of a trinity, of a sweet co-operation between yourself and the two so dear to you: God and a single human being.

For some, that "other" is not a human being: some give themselves directly to God. And, as they kneel at an altar, brides not of men but of Christ, their gift too is a lovely, thrilling thing: the gift of an undivided heart:

> "See, Lord, at thy service low lies here a heart
> Lost, all lost in wonder at the God thou art."[1]

For they have captured and imprisoned a tremendous truth:

[1] Gerard Manley Hopkins, S. Thomae Aquinatis Rhythmus ad SS. Sacramentum "Adoro te supplex, latens deitas," in Poems of Gerard Manley Hopkins, ed. Robert Bridges and W. H. Gardner (London-New York-Toronto: Oxford University Press, 1948), p. 186.

"There is only one sorrow: not to be a saint."[2] And of them too images of Christ are born—not of their bodies but of their souls—of their tears and their prayers, of their striving and straining for young and old, for the sick, the weak, and the wayward.

But, for some, that "other" is not a single human being, and it is not God directly. In our blindness we have chained God's call—vocation—to a kitchen and a cloister. And yet, in His goodness God intended that there should always be women who, for a day or for life, would give themselves, not directly to Him, not to a single human being, but to a whole little world of human beings. We call it a "career"—but the word has been ringed round with selfishness. In point of fact, doctor or lawyer or teacher, social worker, nurse, or psychiatrist, if a woman is to satisfy the deepest demands of her nature, there must always be question of a giving. Not merely pills or opinions or report cards, not merely relief of body or peace of mind. If a woman is to satisfy the deepest demands of her nature, if a woman is to live the blueprint God drew for her on the sixth day of creation, she must give herself, and she must give God.

In brief, God fashioned woman for the giving of life and the life of giving. This means, in the first place, that woman is synonymous with love. There are unsuspected depths in the couplet from Byron's *Don Juan*:

> "Man's love is of man's life a thing apart,
> 'T is a woman's whole existence. . . ."[3]

And a woman lives instinctively what a man must learn painfully: that, whether the object of love be human or divine, to

2 Léon Bloy, *La femme pauvre* (Paris: Mercure de France, 1946), p. 299.

3 Lord Byron, *Don Juan*, Canto 1, 194, *The Works of Lord Byron: Poetry* 6, ed. Ernest Hartley Coleridge (new ed.; London: John Murray; New York: Charles Scribner's Sons, 1903), p. 71.

love is to give; to love perfectly is to give till there is nothing left to give. Only then can two, remaining two, become utterly one.

It means, in the second place, that woman is synonymous with compassion. Her lifelike portrait is Michelangelo's *Pietà*: the lifeless Christ in the arms of His mother. For the Christian woman senses that every human frame is another Calvary, where a human soul is playing out the passion of Christ, making up in his own body, as St. Paul said, "what is wanting to the sufferings" (Col 1:24) of his Lord. She sees that every suffering Christian is Christ suffering, that therefore each Christian whose arms enfold him is Mary.

And because her life is love, because of her capacity for compassion, woman is synonymous with suffering. You see, God shaped a woman's heart for love, and so He made it sensitive and strong: so sensitive, it quivers at the slightest hurt; so strong, it stands by the cross to the end. For a woman's giving is somehow climaxed when, like Eve cradling the cold flesh of Abel, or like Mary beneath the cross, she must give up the object of her love.

That gift of giving—the capacity to give up—is movingly told in the Old Testament. Two women stand before King Solomon. Each has given birth to a baby boy; one infant has died. Each woman claims that the living child is hers. Each cries: "It is *your* child that is dead, *mine* is alive." And Solomon, in his wisdom, asks for a sword. "Cut the living child in two, and give half to one, half to the other." At that, Scripture tells us, "the true mother of the living child, whose heart went out to her son, cried out: 'No, my lord, give *her* the living child; never kill it!' Not so the other: 'Neither mine nor thine,' she said; 'let it be divided between us.' 'No,' said the king, 'do not kill the living child. Give it to the first: she is its mother' " (3 Kgs 3:16–27).

My dear friends: A woman's life is our Lady's life. It recaptures the joyful, the sorrowful, and the glorious mysteries. Her joy is in giving; her sorrow, in giving up; her glory will come when God gives back a hundredfold the love she has lavished on a single human being, on a whole little world of human beings, and on Him.

Sin and Incarnation

6. Disunity: The Price of Sin

IF THERE IS any one word that sums up this mid-century, I suggest it is . . . disunity. If there is any one characteristic that marks our era, it is cleavage, division, separation. This absence of unity, of oneness, displays itself on four levels: between man and nature; within man himself; between man and man; between man and God.

In the first place, there is disunity *between man and nature*. As a thoughtful writer recently put it, "the whole of the material side of life, instead of joining in the praise of God and making life lovely, seems to be moving further and further away from God, to be making life more and more ugly, and to be dragging man down more and more rapidly into defilement and evil."[1] The evidence is in our music, our language, our theatre, our art—in our play, our politics, our advertising, our sex. Science itself is used on a gigantic scale, from drugs to an atom, to make man less divine, less human, even to destroy him. Money, pleasure, beauty, power, success—rarely have these been more perilous possessions. In a word, it is difficult today to discover God in His creation, hard to touch God through the things of God. It is as though the things we see and hear and touch and taste and smell were somehow divorced from the God who fashioned them.

[1] Gerald Vann, *The Water and the Fire* (London: Collins, 1953; New York: Sheed & Ward, 1954), p. 174.

Second, this disunity between man and nature is a symbol, and to some extent an effect, of the disunity that exists *within man himself*. I am one person, yet I am at war with myself. That deep-rooted conflict was described with rare insight by St. Paul in his letter to the Christians of Rome. "My own actions bewilder me; what I do is not what I wish to do, but something which I hate. . . . It is not the good my will prefers, but the evil my will disapproves, that I find myself doing. Inwardly, I applaud God's disposition, but I observe another disposition in my lower self, which raises war against the disposition of my conscience, and so I am handed over as a captive to that disposition towards sin which my lower self contains" (Rom 7:15–23).

Third, this disunity within man himself is a symbol, and to some extent a cause, of the disunity that prevails *between man and man*. Half the human race is at war with the other half. It is not simply a war between nations. A cold war rages between those who have and those who have not, between employer and employee, between white and black, between atheist and believer, between Protestant and Catholic, even at times between a man and the woman who is one flesh with him. A terrifying feature of our times, from the human ashes in a concentration camp to the whispered words of everyday living, is "man's inhumanity to man." Like the pagans of St. Paul's day, men and women whose law of life should be love have turned "ruthless, faithless, pitiless" (Rom 1:31).

Fourth, all these disunities are but a symptom, and in great measure an effect, of the most blasphemous disunity of all: the cleavage *between man and God*. At this instant there are literally millions of pitiable human beings who say in their hearts, "There is no God." There are millions more pitiable still who say in their hearts, "There is a God," yet exile Him from their lives. The fact that is writ large on human society today is that so much of human society apparently does not feel the need of God, does not want God, and so does not have God. And *there* is the heart of the matter—*there* is the root of our disunity. Remember the tragic sentence of Paul: "As they scorned to keep God in their view, so God has abandoned them to a frame of mind worthy of all scorn, that prompts them to disgraceful acts . . . every kind of injustice" (Rom 1:28–29). That is why they are "ruthless, faithless, pitiless."

Here you have the first significant fact: the fact of disunity. The second significant fact: it was not always thus. For a tragically brief period in the story of humanity an incredible unity existed. I mean, when only two human beings were alive —the first two. That unity revealed itself on four levels.

In the first place, a remarkable oneness prevailed, an intimate harmony, *between man and God*. When God made Adam, He gave him not simply a garden of delights, the beasts of the field, the birds of the air, a woman from his flesh. More precious than all, God gave man . . . God. The first instant Adam came from the hand of God, the first moment Eve was fashioned from the flesh of Adam, Father, Son, and Holy Spirit lived within them. Human creation was one with its Creator.

Second, there was a striking unity, a fascinating harmony, *within man himself*: within Adam, within Eve. That grim, unceasing struggle which we experience within ourselves, which Paul described—flesh warring against spirit, emotion against reason, passion against purpose, the unreasoning drives of my lower self and the cold logic of my mind—such conflict did not exist in paradise. Adam, like Eve, could not be taken by surprise, could not be swept away by anger, by hate, by lust. Adam's flesh, like Eve's, was utterly swayed by reason, and Adam's reason bent low before his God.

Third, in God's plan there was to be a unique oneness *between man and man*. In God's providence the harmony within the flesh of Adam was symbolic of, was intended to flower in, an unbelievable harmony among his children till time was swallowed up in eternity. Never war, only peace; not hate, but love; no "mine and thine," only "I and thou."

A final unity God forged *between man and nature*. No sooner had He fashioned Adam and Eve to His own image, no sooner had He gifted them with the power to know and the power to love, than He blessed them: "Increase and multiply, and fill the earth, and subdue it . . ." (Gn 1:28). In God's graciousness mute creation would be eloquent; each "thing" would speak to man of the God who molded it. No starlight but would captivate his mind as it captivated Ignatius; no rose but would ravish his soul as it ravished Teresa. At that moment each blade of grass, each feathered wing, each vein of gold, each breath of air was not a rival, not an enemy, not a reluctant captive, but a willing servant. All nature would minister to man in his growing awareness of God, in his mounting love for his Lord.

Here you have the second significant fact: the fact of unity. The third significant fact: this primitive unity did not endure. It did not survive a single temptation.

When Adam disobeyed God, he created chaos; he destroyed unity. In the first place, he ruptured the bond that linked *man and God*. When love fled from Adam's soul, the God of Love fled with it. The sentence in Genesis is expressive: "[God] cast out Adam, and placed before the paradise of pleasure Cherubim, and a flaming sword turning every way, to keep the way of the tree of life" (Gn 3:24). Man had been exiled from God.

Second, Adam destroyed the harmony *within himself*, the symmetry God had designed for every personality. Till the end of time, men would be lured from God by the devil within them; man's worst enemy would be himself. Flesh would rise up against spirit, spirit against God: "I will not serve." Again, the words of Genesis after the sin of Adam are pregnant: "The eyes [of Adam and Eve] were opened, . . . they perceived themselves to be naked. . . . And the Lord God called Adam . . . and Adam said: I heard thy voice in paradise, and I was afraid, because I was naked, and I hid myself" (Gn 3:7–10). Man was a stranger to himself.

Third, Adam severed the link God had forged *between man and man*, the link of love. In consequence of Adam's sin, the first two brothers in human history went forth to a field, and (Scripture tells us) "Cain rose up against his brother Abel, and slew him" (Gn 4:8). Man had been sundered from man.

Finally, Adam's sin shattered the oneness *between man and nature*. Material creation would conspire against him: the winds and the waves would refuse to obey him, beauty would seduce him and loveliness betray him, animals would turn into enemies or slaves-by-compulsion. The promise God hurled at Adam is fraught with meaning: "Cursed is the earth in thy work; with labor and toil shalt thou eat thereof all the days of thy life" (Gn 3:17).

Here you have the third significant fact: the fact of Adam, of sin. But there is a fourth significant fact: the fact of Christ, of grace. To restore the unity that had been sundered by sin, the Son of God became man. Yes, to recapture in some measure the divine dream of human harmony, to put man at peace with God, with himself, with his fellow man, and with all creation.

With His birth and His death Christ our Lord has destroyed the foundations of disunity; in Bethlehem and on Calvary God Himself began the task of human unity. To begin with, He linked man with God. "All those who welcomed Him He empowered to become the children of God, all those who believe in His name" (Jn 1:12). Second, He made it possible for man to live at peace within himself. Remember the problem of Paul? "Pitiable creature that I am, who is to set me free from a nature thus doomed to death?" Remember his answer? ". . . Jesus Christ our Lord" (Rom 7:24–25). Third, He made it possible for man to live at peace with his fellow man. "A new commandment I give unto you, that you love one another as I have loved you" (Jn 13:34). To realize this love, He gathered us into one body, His own body, with Himself as Head: "You are all one in Christ Jesus" (Gal 3:28). And, finally, He won for us the grace to live in some sort of harmony with material creation—not only with the animal but even with the atom. True, we cannot achieve that utter, unlabored domination which the first man had over the creatures of earth; but we can, if we will, use the things of God to reach God.

I would leave one thought with you. It was *Adam's* sin, yes, that began the process of human disunity; but it is *our* sin, yours and mine, that increases it. Every sin, be it ever so slight, saps the oneness I need with God, with my fellow man, with the things of earth, even within my inmost self. Every sin makes humanity that less human, that less divine. Conversely, there is a genuine contribution, a splendid gift, you can make to peace on earth, to oneness within you and oneness without. You can love God with your whole heart, and you can love every human being as Christ our Lord has loved you.

7. The Christmas Story: Human and Divine

ONCE EACH year we recapture the rapture of the world's greatest love-story. A love-story with a human touch. A *human* touch. For it tells of a Baby shivering in straw. It tells of a wisp of a girl, whose eyes were lit by love, and whose hands laid her Child in a feeding trough. It tells how God trained a choir of angels and set them to sing in the sky: how the first Christmas carols sent shepherd lads scurrying over the hillside to tell the Infant how much they loved Him. It tells how God hung a new star in the sky: a star that brought kings over a desert and onto their knees. And before we tiptoe from the crib we lull the little one to sleep with a lullaby on our lips:

> "Sleep, sleep, my own:
>> Thy mother's arms enfold thee.
> Lo, at thy borning
>> The winds of the morning grow still.
>
> "Sleep, sleep, my child:
>> Bright angels behold thee.
> Now all is peace
>> In the cave on the hill."

There is the *human* beauty of the Christmas story. John the Evangelist saw all that. After all, he had pillowed his head on the heart of Christ at the Supper. From the lips of the dying Christ he had received Mary for his mother. He must have heard from her own lips, he must have thrilled to her tale of that silent, holy night. And yet, when the apostle of love set pen to paper, he wrote the world's greatest love-story in one line: "The Word was made flesh, and dwelt among us" (Jn 1:14).

"The *Word* was made flesh." That line takes the *human* beauty of the Christmas story and links with it the *divine*. On a magic carpet it takes us from the cold stable and carries us back thousands of years to "a paradise of pleasure" (Gn 2:8). It shows us the first man, and the first woman, and the first sin, and the first blush. For the man and the woman whom God had fashioned with His own hands, whom God had made to father and mother the human race and pass on to their children for all time their own birthday gift of grace—God to nestle in the heart of each child at the dawn of life—these two had sinned. And God told them: life would leave their bodies, because love had fled from their souls. No wonder Adam trembled: "I heard thy voice in paradise, and I was afraid" (Gn 3:10).

Satan had ruined God's plan-of-love for man, poisoned humanity at its source. From Cain to Antichrist, men would be born with sin, live in sin, and die from sin. Till time was no more, men would be lured from God by the devil beneath them, by the devil about them, by the devil within them. Time without number would be sculptured in human flesh the *Pietà* no artist can capture: Eve cradling the body of Abel in her arms, unable to understand that for the first time life had gone out of a human being. And the first tears fell. Sin—concupiscence—death: the mess of pottage our first parents purchased with our birthright.

But if there is one thing stronger than sin, it is love. At

that moment, as Adam cowered beneath God's anger—when each one of us hung by a thread over hell—the love of God spoke. God doomed Satan to defeat. "The first man and the first woman," He told the devil, "have betrayed my love. I will raise up a New Man and a New Woman. I will raise a barrier of grace between you and her, between your sin and her Son. He will crush your head."

Only God quite saw the full beauty of that redeeming promise. Only God quite saw how He would shape a child untouched by sin, and call her Mary. How the chalice of her womb would reach to the womb of eternity, and Mary would give to our world not a mere man but a God-man, and call Him Jesus. How the Second Person of the Blessed Trinity, who had always been a Son, would become a Child. How a Child would lead us back to God, because He Himself is God. For, as the Book of Wisdom tells us: "While all things were in quiet silence, and the night was in the midst of her course, thy Almighty Word leapt down from heaven from thy royal throne" (Wis 18:14–15). "The Word was made flesh, and dwelt among us."

You see, Christmas means nothing, unless it means that God pressed upon the sin-scarred, tear-stained face of humanity a passionate kiss of peace. Humanity needed one thing that midnight: humanity needed Christ. Men did not need caroling angels, sleepless shepherds, treasure-laden kings. None of them could give man what man needed most: forgiveness. Only a God-man could do that: plead for man because He Himself is man; plead successfully because He is God.

Why, sure it's lovely that God bent down to man, lovely that God touched this earth so gently. But it's lovely only because He touched the earth with His forgiveness; it's lovely only because the Child had pity on our childishness. In Bethlehem forgiveness was born—the infant-whisper of the dying cry that would thunder over Calvary: "Father, forgive them!" (Lk 23:34). Forget forgiveness, and Christmas is a feeling; forget forgiveness, and the crib matters more than Christ.

What, then, is the purpose of Christmas? What was Christ's own Christmas dream? Simply this. Christ was born to bear other Christs. Christmas is meaningless unless it means not merely God-in-a-stable, but God-in-a-soul, in your soul. Christmas means grace, and grace means that you are Christ-bearers, Christophers in the richest meaning of the word, that you can cry out with St. Paul: "I live, no longer I, but Christ lives in me" (Gal 2:20). Little wonder that you and I, seeing our salvation in swaddling-clothes, can whisper to our God: "I heard thy voice in Bethlehem, and I was glad."

My dear friends: Christmas is the birth of the Son of God on earth. And yet, only the first Christmas took place in a stable; every Christmas since then has taken place in human hearts. Only the first Christmas recorded the birth of Christ in Bethlehem; every Christmas since then is significant in so far as it records the birth or the rebirth of Christ in men. As St. John expressed it: "He came to His own, and His own did not welcome Him. But all who did welcome Him He empowered to become the children of God, all those who believe in His name. Their birth came, not from human stock, not from nature's will or man's, but from God" (Jn 1:11–13). Christmas means for a Christian a loving act of faith: "I believe in Jesus Christ, God's only Son, our Lord, who was conceived of the Holy Ghost, born of the Virgin Mary." Christmas means the wondering whisper of Thomas: "My Lord and my God!" (Jn 20:28).

"The *Word* was made flesh." That line takes the human beauty of the Christmas story and links with it the divine. It puts *God* in the straw, and the hands that hold Him are the hands of the Mother of *God*. The caroling angels are the *servants* of the Child, and the shepherds were *made* by Him. The Christmas star is His toy, and He alone is true King. And man can sing a lullaby to God, because "the *Word* was made flesh, and dwelt among us."

8. The Christmas Paradox

THERE IS a problem to Christmas—a paradox. Some would call it a flat contradiction. One side of the paradox was sung by Christ's angels, His messengers, the midnight of His birth: "Peace on earth to men of good will . . ." (Lk 2:14). *Peace.* The other side of the paradox was preached thirty years later by Christ Himself: "Do not imagine that I have come to bring peace to the earth. I have come to bring a *sword*, not peace" (Lk 12:51).

Strangely enough, history, the story of man, only emphasizes the paradox. On Jesus' birthday, all is peace: a truce lies over the earth, like a blanket of snow upon a battlefield. On Christmas Day the heart of the most heartless will sense an uneasy peace. But the very next morning the cannon will roar once more, old hates will belch forth anew from human hearts, and a world will awaken to remember that there is no peace.

And the Church, like history, points up the paradox. On Jesus' birthday, all is peace: a Child and His mother, drowsy shepherds, caroling angels, kings bent low in adoration. But the very next day the Church in her liturgy sheds the white vestments of peace for robes blood-red. Red for St. Stephen stoned for Christ; red for the Innocents baptized by Herod in blood; red for Thomas à Becket murdered in a cathedral; and all but red for the Apostle John. "I have come to bring a sword."

One clue to the paradox you will discover during Christmas Week. Three days after the birth of the Infant, we honor the death of the Innocents, the first human beings to prove the truth of Christ's claim: "I have come to bring a sword." You see, the Holy Innocents were put to death for one reason: *they looked like Jesus.* Of the baby boys two years and under, any one might have been Jesus; so Herod killed them all. Perhaps there were as few as five; maybe as many as eighty. The number matters not; what does matter is, they were put to the sword because they looked like Jesus. Like all martyrs, they died *for* Christ; unlike any other martyrs, they died *instead* of Christ. The first to die *for* their Lord, yes; but, more thrilling still, the first to die because they *looked like* their Lord!

And that, I insist, is one clue to the Christmas paradox. Because it tells us something about peace, and something about the sword. In the first place, it tells us something about peace. Those little ones who "looked like Jesus" trumpet, more loudly than words, the purpose of Christmas. Christ was born to bear other Christs. Christmas means grace, and grace means that in its sinlessness, in its love, your soul bears a striking resemblance to Christ. You are by grace, by gift, what He is by nature: you are sons and daughters of God. What the early Christian writers never tired of telling: "God became man to make men gods." You may not feel like Christ; you will not see Christ; but the fact remains: in the eyes of God, you do look like Jesus.

The point to remember is this: the peace the angels sang is not simply some uneasy truce, a cease-fire among men. And "men of good will" are not men bubbling over with some manner of good cheer. "Peace to men of good will" means

"God's peace to God's friends." Christmas peace is, above all else, peace between man and God. That midnight, for the first time since man first laughed at God, God smiled upon man. Christmas peace means what St. John murmured in accents of wonder: "He came to His own, and His own did not welcome Him. But all who did welcome Him He empowered to become the children of God, all those who believe in His name" (Jn 1:11–12). The peace the angels sang has rarely been summed up more strikingly than in the simple sentence of St. Paul: "He Himself is our peace" (Eph 2:14). *There* is the peace no human being can take from you, no human being save yourself: Christ is your peace.

In likeness to Christ, then, there is peace: peace with God. But in Christlikeness there is the sword, too. Because they "looked like Jesus," the Innocents suffered and died. And the Herods of this world are on the loose again. Human beings are still being hounded, will always be hounded, if they look like Jesus. Holy Innocents, who are wholly innocent of any crime, save the crime of looking like Christ, of living Christ. From a Stepinac with a pectoral cross that makes the headlines, to the unknown Christian soldier who rots in an unmarked grave or a concentration camp because he dared to resemble his Lord!

I said that only the Innocents died instead of Christ. In a very true sense, *all* martyrs die instead of Christ, in place of Christ. For what the Herods of any age seek to destroy is not so much Christians as Christ. But there is only one way to kill Christ, and that is by killing Christ *in you*. And so, if persecution should ever strike you, Herod will mark for destruction not so much you as the likeness of Christ in you. Few Herods will ever hate you, few Herods will ever fear you, as an individual. What they hate, what they fear, is the image of

Christ in you. The proof? The only thing a martyr has to do in order to live, is to deny the Christ within him, cast out Christ!

It follows, then, that the second half of the Christmas paradox—the sword—can be avoided. Stephen and Sebastian and Agnes, Cecilia and Thomas à Becket: they did not *have* to pour out their blood; they could have cast out Christ instead. And so it is with each of you: you do not have to pay the price of Christian living. You can rebel against a God who makes the wicked to prosper, and lays His hand so heavily on such as seek Him. You can hate and hurt and swear revenge; you can lie and steal and blaspheme; you can refashion gold into a god and transform love into lust. In a word, you can cast out Christ.

And yet, dear friends, there is one truth no Christian dares deny. You cannot refuse the Christian sword without losing the Christmas peace. You cannot cast out Christ and still possess the peace that *is* Christ. In a word, you cannot avoid sorrow without avoiding Christ. You must take the whole paradox, or none of it. If you are to look like Jesus, you may not rest content with the joy thereof; you must bear the anguish as well. That is why my Christmas prayer for you is so unusual, and so real. I do not pray that God may wipe away each tear from your eyes. I pray simply that each day of your lives you may look a little more like Jesus, and that the sorrow that comes of carrying God's cross upon your back may be sweetened by the peace that comes of carrying God Himself within your heart.

9. Nothing under the Sun Is New

THOUSANDS of years ago a wise man—a man wise with the wisdom of God—wrote: "Nothing under the sun is new; neither is any man able to say: Behold this is new. For it hath already gone before us in the days that were before" (Ecclesiastes 1:10). The words of Solomon are especially apt on this birthday of a new year: "No man is able to say: Behold this is new." For the paradox of the New Year is this: there will be very little that is really new.

You see, the same ten commandments will be smashed—more ruthlessly than Moses smashed them on the foot of Mount Sinai—and more casually. For the same good God will be blasphemed and betrayed, denied and crucified again; the same Sacrifice of Calvary will be mocked on our altars. Only they who crucify Him may be different. . . . Human beings will still die from man's inhumanity to man: because they have nothing to eat, nothing to wear, no place whereon to rest their heads; or because barbed wire chokes their will to live. Only the faces will be new. . . . The same impurities will ease the passions of 1960, for much the same reasons, much the same excuses. Only new temples of the Holy Spirit will be desecrated. . . . Thievery will remain a fine art: another's wife, another's goods, another country. Only the prize may be new. . . . Reputations will still disappear: across a yard, over the air, in print. Only the names may be new.

And, looking about you, looking within you, will you dare to predict a sort of mid-century moratorium on sin? Do you think the world of 1960—the Christian world of '60—will awaken to the fact that there are *seven* deadly sins, not *one*? So that there will be in 1960 not merely a lessening of lust, but an end to envy and anger, a slackening of drunkenness and sloth, a repeal of pride and greed? No, I'm terribly afraid Solomon will not exclaim: "Behold, *this* is new!"

And yet, in that very absence of novelty there is salvation. Old facts, new faces. If there will always be much evil in the world, there will always be much holiness. Not a holiness different from the days of Bethlehem: always the same fire of love, only new hearts afire. No new sanctity: only new car- penter-saints, new mothers and fathers and innocents, new shepherds and kings, all with God in their hearts, all aflame with love for the Child in the crib. So that in 1960 even the commandments will take on richness. For every blasphemy, the bent head of some dear soul:

> "See, Lord, at thy service low lies here a heart
> Lost, all lost in wonder at the God thou art."[1]

For every Herod, new innocents; for every Stephen done to death, a St. Paul born of his blood: "for me, life is Christ, and death is gain" (Phil 1:21). For every lustful life, some- where an Aloysius sworn to chastity. For every life blasted by scandalous lips, for every home withered by scandalous lives, somewhere the love that knows no peer: that a man, a Christ, lay down his life for the object of his love. Of such will Solomon say: "Behold, *this* is new!"

Dear friends in Christ: During the Second World War a man said: "I have a little boy. . . . When the war broke out, I was very much distressed about him, because I found I was taking it for granted that life ought to be better and easier

---

[1] St. Thomas Aquinas, *Adoro te*, translated by Gerard Manley Hopkins, *loc. cit.*

for him than it had been for my generation. Then I realized that I had no right to take this for granted at all—that the fight between good and evil must be the same for him as it had always been, and then I ceased to feel so much distressed."[2]

"The fight between good and evil must be the same for him as it had always been." Dear friends in Christ, I do not say there will be no war in 1960; there may be. I do not say there will be no sin; there will be. I do not say, "Be good and you'll be happy"; you may not be. But one thing I do predict: the struggle between good and evil will be joined in your soul this year as every year—as it has been since the temptation of Eve. Whether it takes place on a battlefield or in a classroom, in an office or at home, on a bed of roses or a bed of thorns, on Charles Street in Baltimore or on the Bowery in New York, in the cassock of a priest or the habit of a nun, makes no essential difference. The battle will be joined.

The key to the struggle is given in the Epistle, the biblical text with which the Church begins each new year. The words are the words of St. Paul: "The grace of God, our Saviour, has dawned on human kind, schooling us to forgo irreverent thoughts and worldly appetites, and to live, in this present world, a life of order, of justice, and of holiness. We were to look forward, blessed in our hope, to the day when there will be a new dawn of glory, the glory of our Saviour Jesus Christ, who gave Himself for us, to ransom us from all our guilt, a people set apart for Himself, ambitious of noble deeds" (Titus 2:11–14).

Ponder this in 1960—*do* this in 1960—and not some wise man, not a Solomon, but God Himself will say of *you:* "Behold, *this* is new!"

---

[2] Dorothy L. Sayers, *Creed or Chaos?* (London: Methuen; New York: Harcourt, Brace & Company, 1947), p. 39.

The Life of Christ and
The Life of the Christian

10. The Holy Family

BETHLEHEM was a birthplace—the birthplace of a child. But Bethlehem was more than the birthplace of a child. Bethlehem was the birthplace of a family. When Mary laid the shivering body of Jesus in the cradle of Joseph's arms, the first Christian family was born.

For almost thirty years that family clung together. They fled together to Egypt when Herod baptized the babies of Bethlehem in their own blood. They lived together in a rude village where everyone knew their every secret, save the one big secret—that Jesus was God. They worked together at the hardest and humblest of tasks: Joseph a laborer, Mary a mother, Jesus a boy. Joseph the carpenter kept his loved ones in bread with the skill of his hands. Mary baked and spun, carried water and taught Jesus to pray. Jesus Himself lived a life so utterly simple and natural and human that Nazareth never knew it was housing its God.

That working-family was made up of the three *holiest* persons who ever walked this earth. The holiest was the child—the child whose human nature was the human nature of God—the child who *was* God. Then came the mother—the mother who was closer to her child than any creature ever was or ever will be. And last of all, the father—whose lot in life it was to take care of God and God's mother. Jesus, Mary,

Joseph: in that order. For Mary was molded by God to give us Jesus; and Joseph was chosen by God to cast his rugged arms about both.

But God had raised up a *family*. And as in every family, so too in the Holy Family, the father was head of the house, the mother was his helpmate and its heart, and the child—the child bowed His head before both. Joseph, Mary, Jesus: in that order. Jesus, who had framed the world out of nothing, learned from Joseph how to turn out a plow. Jesus, who was Himself the God of Love, learned from Mary how to love God. Jesus, whom the angels obey, took orders from two of His own creatures. And God the Father smiled His pleasure from heaven.

But God had raised up a *human* family. And so one day Jesus and Mary folded the lifeless hands of Joseph on his breast—and loneliness lay over Nazareth. One spring afternoon Mary waved to her Son as He disappeared round the bend, bound for souls and a cross at the end; one spring afternoon the mother who first cradled the naked body of her baby in a stable, last cradled that same naked body beneath a cross —and loneliness lay over Jerusalem. And one lovely evening the Mother of God, grown old as gracefully as the petals fall from the rose, left this earth; and the Son who had come from her without pain, without pain folded her forever to His sacred breast.

My dear friends: The paradox of Nazareth is this: the Holy Family did not die with Jesus, Mary, and Joseph. *Every* family is a *holy* family. You see, the first vocation on God's earth was a vocation to marriage, God's call to a family. A holy vocation, for the hand of God was lifted in blessing as He murmured: "Increase and multiply, and fill the earth" (Gn 1:28). A holy vocation, for in the eyes of God the union between husband and wife is a sacred symbol: it signifies, it illustrates, the unbreakable bond that links Christ and His Church. A holy vocation, for the Son of Mary blessed a bride and groom at Cana, and the water blushed to wine at His blessing. A holy vocation, for the Son of God raised marriage between Christians to the dignity of a sacrament: hand-in-hand they kneel at the altar, and husband gives to wife, wife gives to husband, the wedding gift of grace—God to dwell in each other's soul. A holy vocation, because in Bethlehem God changed the meaning of mother: ever since Bethlehem every Christian mother is another Mary, because the fruit of her womb is another Christ.

But if it is to be truly holy, the family must never cease to be a *family*. And that means: in each family, as in the Holy Family, there must be one and the same principle of family life: subjection softened by love. The idea has never been put more powerfully than in the breathtaking paragraph where St. Paul compares husband and wife to Christ and His Church:

"Wives must obey their husbands as they would obey the Lord. The man is the head to which the woman's body is united, just as Christ is the head of the Church—He the Saviour on whom the safety of His body depends. Why then, women must owe obedience at all points to their husbands, as the Church does to Christ.

"You who are husbands must show love to your wives, as Christ showed love to the Church when He gave Himself up on its behalf. He would hallow it, purify it . . . summon it into His own presence . . . in all its beauty, no stain, no wrinkle, no disfigurement. . . . And that is how husband ought to love wife, as if she were his own body; in loving his wife, a man is but loving himself. It is unheard of that a man should bear ill will to his own flesh and blood. No, he keeps

[59]

it fed and warmed. . . . Each of you is to love his wife as he would love himself, and the wife is to pay reverence to her husband" (Eph 5:22–33).

Reverence. . . . Reverence for each other means reverence for another—reverence for that image of themselves which is at the same time the full flowering, the incarnation, of their love, and, like Jesus, subject to them. I mean, reverence for a child, for their child, as the masterwork of a trinity, of a sweet co-operation between man and woman and God. You see, it is not simply society that the family builds, but the Body of Christ. As the first Holy Family built up so tenderly the physical body of their little Christ, so every holy family since then is divinely destined to build up the Mystical Body of Christ, the Church that is the continuation of Christ down the ages. That is why we reverence, why we cultivate the child—mind and heart, body and soul—as a being wonderfully and fearfully made, a blend of the animal and the angel, into whose growing must go the strength of a father, the tenderness of a mother, and the grace of God. Only thus does the home become an image of Nazareth, with its own trinity: its own Joseph, its own Mary, its own little Jesus.

And yet, as at Nazareth, so every holy family is a very *human* thing. It was made to be *one*: like Jesus and Mary and Joseph, it was made to live together, to work together, to play and pray together, even to flee together. And in that oneness, somehow—somewhere—God touches this troubled world with His peace. But the family is a very human thing. In God's wisdom it is not unchangeably one. Till the end of time—all over the earth—Jesus and Mary will fold the hands of Joseph lovingly on his breast. Till the end of time other Christs will leave Nazareth, leave it lonelier, because they have another and perhaps a richer love in their hearts. Till the end of time Mary will be inexpressibly lonely. It is simply the shadow of the cross brooding over every Nazareth. And in that shadow, in the agony of separation as in the ecstasy of union, God's blessing breathes upon us and upon the world. "His will is our peace."[1]

Let me leave one last thought with you. Every holy family, I said, was made to be one. The fact is: one day every holy family will be one. Unchangeably one. As Jesus and Mary and Joseph are one. The day when God will wipe away all tears from our eyes and murmur:

> "All which I took from thee I did but take,
> Not for thy harms,
> But just that thou might'st seek it in My arms.
> All which thy child's mistake
> Fancies as lost, I have stored for thee at home:
> Rise, clasp My hand, and come!"[2]

[1] Dante, Divina commedia: Paradiso, Canto 3.

[2] Francis Thompson, "The Hound of Heaven," in Francis Thompson, Poems and Essays, ed. Wilfred Meynell (Westminster, Md.: The Newman Press, 1949), p. 112.

11. ⚜ I Have Compassion on the Crowd

AMONG OUR Lord's recorded words, there is one particularly touching phrase. As He looks out over the hungry thousands —men and women who have been with Him three days and have nothing to eat—He says to His disciples: "I have compassion on the crowd" (Mt 15:32).

"I have compassion." That expression runs like a golden thread through the Gospel, through the life of Christ. He sees the crowds "bewildered and dejected, like sheep without a shepherd," and, St. Matthew tells us, "He was moved with compassion for them" (Mt 9:36). He sees another large crowd and "out of compassion for them" (Mt 14:14) He heals their sick. Two blind men cry, "Have mercy on us!", and "moved with compassion for them" (Mt 20:30, 34) He opens their eyes. A leper pleads, "If you want to, you can make me clean," and "having compassion on him" (Mk 1:40–41) Jesus stretches forth His hand. Because a father begs, "Have compassion on us and help us" (Mk 9:21), He drives a devil out of a lad. Because a mother weeps, the Lord has "compassion on her" (Lk 7:13) and gives life to her only son.

Three of His best-loved stories are tales of compassion. The master who forgives his servant a tremendous debt because he is "moved with compassion" (Mt 18:27). The Good Samaritan who binds up the wounds of a Jew fallen among robbers because he is "moved with compassion" (Lk 10:33). And the father who kisses his prodigal son in total forgiveness because he is "moved with compassion" (Lk 15:20).

Briefly, the Gospels portray God-in-flesh "moved with compassion" for all manner of suffering: for the sick, the hungry, and the debtor; for the blind and the bewildered; for the sinner and the bedeviled; for the leper touched by God and the Jew struck by men; for a mother.

And the reason for it all is quite obvious; St. Paul has chiseled it in deathless language: "We have not a high priest who cannot have compassion on our infirmities, but one tried as we are in all things except sin" (Heb 4:15). It's a startling thought, isn't it? The Son of God took human flesh of Mary; He took for Himself our nature. But, not more my nature than yours; not more your nature than the nature of the Roman called Herod or the Jew whose name was Judas. In fact, the Son of God took human flesh "to save what was lost" (Mt 18:11). The farther the sheep had strayed, the lower the prodigal had sunk, the greater was the challenge to His love. The more repulsive the body to human liking, the deeper was His yearning to make lovely the soul within with His indwelling.

No, the problem is not with God; the problem lies with us. God is rich in compassion—compassion not merely for material suffering, but compassion in every age for the Judas who sells Him for silver and the Peter who denies Him with an oath; for the Herod who mocks Him for a fool and the Pilate who washes his hands of Him; for the servant who slaps His cheek and the soldier who digs deep holes in His hands and feet.

The problem of compassion lies with us. So much of the world's sickness stems from this, that human beings are without compassion. Look about you. You have the paradox of the Communist, who would help his fellow man without loving him, and, as St. Paul remarked of the pagan of his day, being godless he is "ruthless, faithless, pitiless" (Rom 1:31). You have the scandal of so many unbridled capitalists, whose dogma is "dog eat dog." Not so long ago you had the post-war battle cry: "Let the Germans starve—they have brought it on themselves!" And always you have the bias against displaced persons, refugees, immigrants: "Let the shiftless shift for themselves!" You have all the petty hatred, all the petty bigotry, all the petty meanness that shrinks our hearts, poisons our minds, and defiles our tongues.

Recently a book reached this country. It is made up of letters written by soldiers. Not American soldiers, but Japanese—most of them members of the Special Attack Corps, the Kamikaze, or, as we used to call them, the "suicide pilots." One of them was killed in the battle for Okinawa. His age was twenty-one. The letter was to his mother, two days before he flew off to attack units of the U. S. Fleet. In it he said:

"I am writing this letter expecting my final mission the day after tomorrow. . . . Once in a while I think that I would like to come home beside you—but this is of course a very bad thing to think about. When I was baptized I was told to 'die,' was I not? And I was also told that, even if I were killed by a bullet shot by an American soldier, I would die in the hands of my Saviour. Now I remember those words very clearly. Yes, everything is in the hands of God. Life or death does not matter in this world when guided by God, does it, Mother? Isn't it true that Jesus prayed, 'Be it done unto me according to thy word'? I read the Bible every day, because when I am reading it I feel like I am with you. I will dive into the American fleet with the Bible and my Hymnal. . . ."

My dear friends: One thing I am sure of: looking on that young Japanese, Christ our Lord would have been moved with compassion. One thing I am not so sure of: are *we*?

You know, perhaps the Greeks of old were not so far wrong when they situated compassion, pity, mercy deep within our bodies; and it is interesting to find old Zachary in the New Testament extolling "the bowels of the mercy of our God" (Lk 1:78). It is not the physiology that matters; it is the realization that compassion is not of pocketbook dimensions, that compassion is born of our inmost selves, of our love.

If I love God, I will have compassion on His image; and the image of God is man—every man. It is the image of God that is somehow defaced by war and sin and hunger and hatred and even bewilderment. Each of you is as much a missionary as Paul or Francis Xavier, a missionary to the world you enter each day, a little world with more colors, more costumes, more smells than Paul or Xavier ever dreamed of. You may not be called to reap the harvest, but you are asked to plant the seed: a gracious word to this cripple, a kindness to this beggar, a quiet prayer that this human being, so ruthless, so faithless, so pitiless, may soon be one with the rest of us.

For that I need God's grace. Let me pray, then, that I too may come to "have compassion on the crowd"; that, like the Christ of crowds, I too may come to care no more for the color, the clothes, the smell of a human being than I care for the rough wrapping round a priceless package.

At any rate, in my lack of compassion, let me not boast that I am less Christian than Christ.

12. The Kingship of Christ

And Pilate asked Jesus: Art thou, then, a king?
And Jesus answered: Thou sayest it: I am a king.

(Jn 18:37)

My dear friends: The scene I have stolen from the Gospel of John recalls a startling truth about Jesus of Nazareth. It reminds us that this child shivering in straw, this carpenter handling a saw, this Jew tramping a dusty lane, this convict quivering in pain—it reminds us that this man is King of the universe. Oh, it's true, this child first opened His eyes in a stable—and yet the prophet Isaias could announce: "A child is born to us, but the sceptre of a king is upon His shoulder" (Is 9:6). This carpenter earned His bread in the sweat of His brow—and still Daniel could prophesy: "God gave Him power and glory and a kingdom, and all peoples, tribes, and tongues shall serve Him" (Dan 7:14). This Jew whispered the secret of His gospel in a tiny corner of the world—and still the Psalmist sang: "He shall rule from sea to sea, and from the river unto the ends of the earth" (Ps 71:8). This convict died with nails in His flesh—but an angel had told His mother: "Of His kingdom there shall be no end" (Lk 1:33).

But how can this be? How can this crucified Jewish carpenter, this child of Mary, how can He be King of the universe? Simply: because He is what He is, and because He did what He did! Christ is King because He is what He is: not a mere man, but the God-man, God-with-us, God in human flesh. And Christ is King because He did what He did: He purchased us "at a great price" (1 Cor 6:20). For, as St. Peter insisted, "you were redeemed not with perishable things, with silver or gold, but with the precious blood of Christ, as of a lamb without blemish and without spot" (1 Pt 1:18–19). He bought us with His blood, so much so that, in the language of St. Paul, "your very bodies are members of Christ" (1 Cor 6:15). He is King because He is what He is: the God-man. And He is King because He did what He did: He bought us with His blood.

And this kingship, this dominion of Christ is universal. There is *nothing* that is not His: "All power," He insisted, "All power has been given to me—in heaven and on earth" (Mt 28:18). That is why the planets are His playthings, and the wavelets on the water the gentle ripple of His will. And there is *no one* who is not His. He is your King and He is mine. He is Head of your home, and His heart must be enthroned therein. He is our country's King—every country's King—even if she claim to have "no king save Caesar." And our president's solitary boast should be that he rules not by his own right, but by the mandate and in the place of a divine King—that his authority mirrors the authority of Christ.

Yes, Christ our Lord is King. He owns us, body and soul. He has a right to command, and we—we have an obligation to obey. And yet, dear friends, the dominion of Christ over men is something new in the relation between a ruler and his subjects. "My kingdom," He said, "is not of this world" (Jn 18:36). It is not like the kingdoms *you* know. You see, this King had pity on His subjects, and so He stepped down from heaven and put on our flesh. He walked and worked and slept; He learned what hunger tastes like, and thirst; He preached and He prayed; He was sold for silver, slapped and spat upon, whipped like a dog, and nailed to a tree. This King died that His subjects might live—those who love Him and those who hate Him. This King welcomes you into His kingdom on earth by pouring into you His own divine life. He knows that "it is not by bread alone that man lives" (Mt 4:4), and so He feeds you with His flesh, for otherwise "you will not have life in you" (Jn 6:54)—at least, not God's life. This King is offended a thousand times a day; and He has thousands of other Christs—someone everywhere—whose whole purpose in life is not to punish sin but to communicate His forgiveness. This King hides His kingliness in a semblance of bread; He erects His throne behind a veil. And yet He refuses to be distant from you: by the grace that races through your soul He unites Himself so intimately with you that He can say: "I am the head; you are my body. I am the vine; you are the branches" (Jn 15:5; cf. Eph 1:22-23).

No, this King is not like the kings of earth. You are His slave, and He treats you like a friend. You were dust, and He lifted you a little below the angels. You were homeless, and He gave you His Church; orphans, and He gave you His Father and His mother; hungry, and He gave you His body. You were His enemy, and He died for you.

Why? Because the kingdom of Christ is not like the kingdoms *we* know. The devil—the creature Christ called "the prince of this world" (Jn 16:11)—"took Him to a very high mountain, showed Him all the kingdoms of the world and the glory of them" and said: "All these will I give you . . ." (Mt 4:8–9). And Christ our Lord waved him away. . . . His own countrymen tried to take Him by force and crown Him King of Israel, and He fled up a mountain, alone. . . . Had He said "yes"—to devil or to men—there would have been no Calvary. But His kingdom is not of this world. What this King wants most—even at the cost of crucifixion—what this King wants most is the only thing you can really refuse Him, the one thing He will never take from you unless you give it to Him: and that is your love. Oh, of course He lays down laws —like any true king. But He does not send legions of angels to see that you keep them. He merely murmurs: "If anyone *love* me, he will keep my word, and my Father will love him, and we will come to him and make our home with him" (Jn 14:23).

And yet, dear friends, the dominion of Christ makes demands upon you—strange demands. It demands that you reproduce in your own life the life of your King. It demands, in the first place, an incarnation: that you identify yourself, make yourself one, as He did, with all the living, struggling, suffering, dying men and women who people your life; that you give your heart's affection to all men, because all of them, whether they look like it or not, were redeemed by the same flow of blood that gave you life; in a word, in His word, that you "love one another as I have loved you" (Jn 13:34).

The dominion of Christ demands, in the second place, a hidden life, after the manner of His own—because, strangely enough, the life that is most effective for bending other necks to the sweet yoke of Christ is the life within you, the life no one sees, the life that is a secret between you and the God who is throned in your soul.

And the dominion of Christ demands, as proof of devotion, crucifixion—pain of body and pain of soul. It demands that your tears be mingled with the tears of Christ, the water with the wine, in the one chalice, the chalice of suffering— what He Himself told two discouraged disciples: "Did not the Christ—[does not every Christ]—*have* to suffer these things and *so* enter into His glory?" (Lk 24:26).

The point is: the kingship of Christ, His dominion over men, is not yet perfect—even His rule over your life and mine. It will only be perfect when, as St. John tells us, "death shall be no more, neither shall there be mourning, nor crying, nor pain any more: for God will brush away every tear from your eyes" (Ap 21:4).

13. A Christian Is Another Christ

IN CHRISTIAN thought there is a tremendous truism: "A Christian is another Christ." Vague, isn't it, and distressingly pious? Yes—unless you realize just what Christ was.

There are two sides to Christ. Christ our Lord was (1) fully human, and (2) more than human. He was fully human. On that point Scripture is quite uncompromising: He was like us in all things, sin alone excepted. There was nothing eccentric about Christ: He did not live, like Diogenes, in a tub, on a pillar like Simon Stylites. He was a Jew of His time, a Jew of Palestine. He was born of a Jewish maiden and He died five miles from His manger. He came, in His own words, "eating and drinking" (Mt 11:19). He came to Cana for a wedding, to Bethany for a burial. He ate with respectable folk like Martha and with outcasts like Matthew. He felt at home with everyone: not only with Peter's mother-in-law, but with the Mary who had seven devils and the Samaritan woman who had five husbands. Children curled up in His arms and grown men like Nicodemus talked far into the night with Him.

He could grow angry—angry enough to whip traffickers from a temple. But He could sympathize too: with a widow who had lost her son to God, with a youngster who had lost his inheritance to harlots. He looked on a rich young man and loved him; He looked on a poor young man and raised him

[73]

from the dead. And twice He wept: over Jerusalem and over Lazarus, over His city and His friend.

He knew the thoughts of shepherds and farmers and fisherfolk. He spoke the language of His people. He spoke of sparrows and lilies, of war and peace. He worked with His hands; He learned what hunger tastes like, and thirst; He was tired enough to sleep out a storm in an open boat. He knew what it meant to flee for His life—to be cursed and spat upon. And He left the cross as He had come to the crib: naked, and all but alone.

No, there was nothing eccentric about Christ. He was like us in all things: He was fully human. And yet Christ was more than human. Not simply because He was God. His life is a living proof that human life can be thoroughly human and yet lived on a level *above* the human. In His every action— whether He came eating and drinking, or preaching and praying, living or dying—in His every action there shone a love that was not born of man. His life was a living lesson in His own "two great commandments": love God with your whole heart, love your fellow man as you love yourself. His life, human as it was, was one long act of love that found its consummation in crucifixion: crucifixion for the objects of His love—crucifixion for every human being who has ever come or ever will come into this world.

What followed? Christ was a living, breathing question mark, an inescapable challenge. In His public life Christ could not be disregarded. And He intended it to be so. He intended that every human being who touched the hem of His garment or looked into His eyes or caught the music or thunder of His voice should put a question to himself: "Is this for me? Is this the way human life was meant to be lived? Is this fascinating marriage of the human and the more-than-human—is this what is lacking to my life?"

And there, I submit, lies your vocation as Catholic laymen. If you are to play Christ to the modern world, you must be (1) fully human and (2) more than human. You must be fully human and completely Christian.

You must be fully human. You see, a Catholic is not necessarily queer. He is not necessarily ill at ease in his environment. In fact, you should be as much at ease in your little world as Christ our Lord was in His. And I believe you are. You live now the life of a man, a twentieth-century Maryland man, as naturally as Christ lived the life of first-century Palestine. You work and you dance, you eat and you sleep, you sorrow and you laugh, you are moved to anger and to pity, you are quick to be hurt and a little slower to forgive, you marry or you don't, you vote as you please, and statistics show very little difference between you and your fellow men.

And yet you are, you must be, different. Because your life, human as it is, is more than human. Each act of yours, so much like any other man's act, is transformed by a love that is not born of man—a love of God above all else and a love of men as God's images on earth. Your life is familiar and it is mysterious. It is familiar because it is so similar to other men's lives. It is mysterious because it is so dissimilar. There is a lilt to your laughter and a joy at the inmost core of your sorrow that is intelligible only in terms of love—a love that is literally "out of this world." You have God in your hearts and your hearts are restless till He rests in every man's heart. You must be different because men must say of you what they said of the first Christians: "Look, how they love!" Look how they love God—how they love one another—how they love us!

Fully human and completely Christian. What follows? You are a question mark that cannot be avoided—a living, breathing, perennial challenge to the little world in which you live. Because you are the same and yet you are different. Both are necessary. Your life must be fully human, else men will say: "This life is too different from my own to have any meaning for me." And it must be more than human, thoroughly Christian, else men will say: "This life is not different enough from my own to pose a problem for me." Then, and only then, will your life, like the life of Christ, prove a problem, an inescapable challenge, to all who come into contact with you. Then, and only then, will they be compelled to ask: "Is this for me? Here is a life thoroughly human, and yet more than human. Here is a familiar life, and still it is mysterious. I understand it, and it puzzles me. Is this the way human life was meant to be lived?"

My dear friends: As I offered the Sacrifice of the Mass this morning, I asked the Christ who was Himself so fully human and yet more than human, to complete in you the work which your baptism began in you—to make you day by day more fully human and more completely Christian.

14. The Faculty of Christian Judgment

EVERY HUMAN being exercises the faculty of judgment. Every human being says, "This is so," or, "That is not so"; "This is good," or, "That is bad"; "This should be done," or, "That should not be done." Every human being passes judgment—on great issues and on small—on a whimsical thing like the weather, or on a more significant concern like the "cold war." Every human being passes judgment on the passing human scene. But the heart of the matter is this: In the light of what principle, in the light of what reality, will you exercise the faculty of judgment?

Broadly speaking, there are three realities in the light of which men can, and men do, pass judgment. In the first place, men can, and men do, pass judgment in the light of *man*— isolated man—this concrete human animal on this concrete inhuman earth. It is the dictum of Protagoras: "The measure of all things is man." Now that man, in the light of whom I judge all things, may be myself or it may be my fellow man. It may be my own self; I can judge the human scene in the light of the satisfaction I personally get or fail to get out of something. War with China would be bad, because a foxhole on Formosa is the death of my ambitions. Or, war with China would not be bad at all, because I am an atomic physicist, and war is the hen to hatch my golden eggs. That man, in the light of whom I judge all things, may be my fellow man. Should we attack and destroy Russia now? Yes, if we are to leave a legacy of peace to generations yet unborn. Should we starve our prisoners of war, rack them, kill them? Why not? After all, the enemy is doing as much to our boys.

And the mainsprings that motivate these judgments are legion. Some judgments spring from fear: Every Red must stand up and be counted, otherwise we perish. Some spring, touchingly, from love: Bring our sons back from overseas; we cannot bear the tears of separation. Some spring from sheer reason: I have nothing left to live for; therefore, the sensible thing is to scatter my brains over a pavement. In any event, in all these judgments the measure is man: myself, or the human beings who make up the object of my love or of my hate.

Please understand me. I am not denying the norm of natural morality. I am not denying that the rule of ethical conduct (as we teach it in our Catholic colleges) is human nature in its completeness. In that sense, the measure of all things *is* man. But there are two things I *am* saying. I insist that to judge things in the light of the satisfaction they give me or my fellow man is not at all to judge in the light of human nature in its completeness. It leaves out at least one radical relationship: the relation of man to his God. And I insist further that even to judge things in the light of full natural morality is not enough, simply because it is natural. Man dares not live on ethics alone, because ethics takes you so far and no further. Powerful as it is, ethics, sheer reason, is powerless to portray human nature in its completeness. It is powerless to portray the length and breadth, the height and depth, the sheer sweep of your relationships to yourself, to your fellow man, and to your God, because ethics, sheer reason, does not know all you really are, all your fellow man is, all the true God is.

In the second place, men can, and men do, pass judgment in the light of an *ideology*. You take something relative—an idea, a catchword, an institution—and you elevate it to the status of an absolute. Some men judge everything in the light of democracy. The Catholic Church is alien to America, because the Catholic Church is undemocratic. The argumentation is simple and rather plausible. In the Catholic Church the people have no voice—no voice as to whom they are to obey, what they are to do, what they must believe; therefore the Church is undemocratic; therefore the Church is alien to democratic America; therefore, in America at least, the Church must be democratized or disappear.

The extreme nationalist, the chauvinist, will judge all things in the light of patriotism. Many men carry in their hearts today what a New York tabloid carried for years on its editorial page, the slogan, the shibboleth of Stephen Decatur: "By the grace of God, may my country be always right —but, my country, right or wrong!"

Or, your ideology may be, "you have to be broadminded." But it is hardly broadminded to claim that any one institution, any one Church, has a corner, a monopoly, on God's revelation; therefore that claim must be false.

Or, your ideology may be, "You have to be modern, up-to-date." But it is not modern to say with St. Paul: "Wives, be subject to your husbands, as the Church is to Christ" (Eph 5:24). It is not up-to-date to spawn children in India, when India cannot feed the children she has. The twentieth century does not believe in hell; therefore hell does not exist.

Or, your ideology may be, "an eye for an eye, and a tooth for a tooth." That is why, in the Second World War, the chairman of the War Writers' Board warned us that we must hate or go under; that is why he confessed, "I hate Germans, and am not ashamed of it"; that is why he told you frankly that, if you think you can hate the sin and love the sinner, if you kill your enemy and claim you love him, you are a hypocrite.

Or, finally, your ideology may be the community standard: "Everybody does it." The best people in my community send their boys to Princeton, their girls to Smith; therefore that is the thing to do.

Again, understand me. I have no quarrel at the moment with democracy or patriotism, with broadmindedness or modernity or the community, even with the Ivy League or its female counterpart. But I do insist that, to take a man-made idea, a man-made slogan, a man-made institution, and make that the ultimate norm of your judgments, is to transform something relative into an absolute, to make a god out of a creature, to worship a golden calf. And that, my friends, is a long step towards blasphemy.

But there is a third way in which men can, and men do, pass judgment. The Christian can, and the Christian must, exercise the faculty of *Christian* judgment. It is simply a question of seeing things through the eyes of God, and of judging things in the light of God. It stems from a fact and a realization. The fact is the Christian fact, the fact of Christ. The realization is this, that the most significant petition in the Our Father is not, "Give us this day our daily bread," nor even, "Forgive us our trespasses," but, "Thy will be done on earth, as it is in heaven." It is the task of the Christian, it is your task, to cast upon human events the judgment God Himself passes on them.

After all, our very philosophy, sheer reason, brings us to the brink, the lip, of that discovery. Natural theology proves that there is such a Being as God, that all other being, all other life, is simply a sharing in the Life, the Being that is God. Ontology insists that this God is the most real of all beings. Cosmology shows that our material universe, lifeless yet quivering with energy, came from the hand of God, that it fulfils God's dream for it by recapturing His perfection imperfectly. Psychology discloses a human soul that can defy time and space, a masterwork of divinity, with intimations of immortality—I mean, a mind restless for the Truth that is a divine Person, a will athirst for the Good that is God. And ethics reveals that man's rational nature is itself a little revelation: with our own minds we can to some extent discover in time what has been the mind, the will of God from eternity.

But there philosophy leaves us. It leaves us in somewhat the state of St. Augustine, as he describes it magnificently in his *Confessions*. He read, he tells us, some books of the Platonists. "In them I found [what we read in St. John] that 'in the beginning was the Word, and the Word was God; all things were made by Him; in Him was life and the life was the light of men.' But I did not read in those books that He came unto His own, and His own received Him not, but to as many as received Him He gave power to be made the sons of God.' I found that the Son 'thought it not robbery to be equal with God,' because by nature He was God; but these books did not tell me that 'He emptied Himself, taking the form of a servant'; that 'He humbled Himself, becoming obedient unto death.' I read there that 'of His fullness souls receive'; I did not read that 'He died for the ungodly,' that 'those who labor and are burdened should come to Him,' that 'the meek He directs in judgment, and the gentle He teaches His ways.' "[1]

[1] St. Augustine, *Confessions* 7, 9; translated by F. J. Sheed, *The Confessions of St. Augustine* (New York: Sheed & Ward, 1943), pp. 142-44.

No, philosophy does not tell us that. You see, it is not the wisdom of men that has made Christian judgment possible and imperative; it is the Wisdom of God, the Word made flesh, Christ Jesus. That is the Christian fact, and it is simply told. God became man to *do* something and to *say* something. He became man to do something: to recapture man's heart by a crucifixion. And He became man to say something: to recapture man's mind by a revelation.

Ever since those gracious days the Christian is no longer at liberty to look at life merely through the eyes of men. At this moment each of you has the eyes of God. We call it faith; but call it what you will—it is simply the power to see life somewhat as God sees it, the power to make a judgment which has for the guarantee of its truth not that *I see* it is so but that *God says* it is so.

Does it make a difference? Think. A philosopher, an Aristotle, can tell us that God is One; only the Christian, and the most illiterate Christian, can insist that God is Three. The philosopher can prove that God is a Creator, and man is a creature; the Christian claims that God is a Father, that we are by grace what Christ is by nature: we are sons of God. The psychologist says that there is something spiritual about his soul, because it has no admixture of matter; the Christian cries that there is something divine about his soul, because it is the dwelling place of divinity. Ethics demands: Love your fellow man as you love yourself; Christianity lays before you the command of Christ: "Love one another as I have loved you" (Jn 13:34). Philosophy tells you that your fellow man is a human person, with the rights and privileges of a person; faith assures you that your fellow man is a person in whom God rests, or else God is restless until He does rest in him.

So, then, in the light of what reality will you, mature Christians, pass judgment on the passing human scene? Briefly, in the light of the reality that is Christ. A new thing, a new life, came into this world twenty centuries ago; that new thing, that new life, is within you, within each one of you, at this moment. Twenty centuries ago it transformed human living; today it has transformed you. Because of it you are a new kind of creature, and therefore different. Deep within you, you have the life of Christ, like another bloodstream. And deep within you—thanks ultimately to the graciousness of God—deep within you, you have the mind, the attitude, the judgment of Christ. Your growth in Christian maturity will be measured in days to come by your growth in Christian judgment—by your ability and your willingness to focus on human events not the eyes of man but the eyes of Christ.

The Eucharist and the Passion

15. The Last Supper: A Challenge to Love[1]

WHEN CHRIST our Lord sat down to His Last Supper, three problems confronted Him. You know what a problem is. Very simply, a problem means: two facts in conflict. On the eve of His crucifixion, three problems confronted Christ, three challenges to His love.

The first problem was this: He had to go, and He wanted to stay. He had to leave us: it was His Father's will. "The Son of Man goes His way," He said, "for so it has been ordained" (Lk 22:22). "It is better for you that I go. For if I do not go, the [Holy Spirit] will not come to you; but if I go, I will send Him to you" (Jn 16:7). He had to leave us; and yet He wanted to stay with us. "My delights are to be with the children of men" (cf. Prv 8:31). And never had He loved His own so intensely as in that hour: "I have longed and longed to share this supper with you before I suffer" (Lk 22:15). There you have it: the bitter anguish of two loves—two loves in conflict. Which will yield? The Father's will? Impossible: "The things that please Him I do always" (Jn 8:29). His love for men: will that have to yield?

With all the power of His divine intellect, with all the

---

[1] For the basic insight and outline of this sermon, and in some of its details, I am indebted to a splendid meditation in G. Longhaye, S.J., *Retraite annuelle de huit jours d'après les Exercices de saint Ignace* (4th ed.; Paris-Tournai: Casterman, 1932), pp. 397–404.

tenderness of His human heart, Christ cuts through the problem with a solution that almost shocks us—a solution that did shock the good folk of Capharnaum. Neither love will have to yield. He will go, and He will stay; He will leave us, and He will remain with us. He will take from His disciples, He will take from us—because the Father wills it—the sensible charm of His presence. No longer will men see His face, hear the music and the thunder of His voice; no longer will they sense the fascination of His smile or be touched by His tears. In that sense He will go: the sensible charm of His presence. And still He will stay: till the end of time He will leave with us the truth of that presence.

Listen to His words: "This is my body. . . . This is my blood" (Mt 26:26, 28). It looks like bread, it feels like bread, it tastes like bread; but it is not bread—it is His body. As long as *this* remains *this*, as long as what looks like bread continues to look like bread, so long will He remain: His real body, His real blood, and everything inseparable from it—His soul, His divineness.

The first problem? He had to go, and He wanted to stay. The solution? He did go, and He did stay. He took from us the God-man as Palestine saw Him with the eyes of the body; He left with us the same God-man, whom you and I see with the eyes of our faith. The solution is simply the Real Presence: He is *present* in the Blessed Sacrament, and His presence is *real*.

The second problem. Once again we have two facts that clash. The first fact is the urgency of love. To love is to give; to love perfectly is to give till there is nothing left to give. Jesus knew it: "Greater love than this no man hath, that a man lay down his life for his friends" (Jn 15:13). Death is the final effort of love, its masterpiece, its triumph. To give till you can give no more, that is love's finest hour, that is love's incredible joy. And so Christ our Lord, whose love for us was beyond human knowing, would gladly have died a thousand deaths for us, would gladly have died daily.

That is the first fact, the urgency of love. The second fact, the fact that clashes with the first, is the tragedy of love. Love cannot die daily, love cannot really die a thousand times. A man can die no more than once for the object of his love. "It is appointed for men once to die" (Heb 9:27). Oh, yes, God can suspend that law by a miracle. After all, Jesus raised the daughter of Jairus to life, the widow's son, the rotting corpse of Lazarus. They died twice. But that is not for the ordinary run of men; that was not for Jesus. His Father wants Him to taste death once. As St. Paul put it: "Christ, having risen from the dead, dies no more" (Rom 6:9).

How does He solve that problem? As before, so now, He cuts through the problem with a solution that almost shocks us—a solution that has shocked thousands through the ages. Of course He can die but once; because the Father so wishes, He will taste but once the bitter joy of bloody death, of blood-red sacrifice. But what a revenge He invents for that deep-seated, unsatisfied desire to die each day for us! "Jesus took bread, blessed it, broke it, gave it to His disciples: 'This is my body.' Taking the cup, He gave thanks, and gave it to them: 'This is my blood'" (Mt 26:26–28). And He added those eternally significant words: "Do this in remembrance of me" (Lk 22:19). To His priests down the ages, till time be no more: Do this: take within your spotless hands a lifeless loaf, and breathe into it the Bread of Life. Do this: take between your trembling fingers a cup of wine, and bathe it with my blood.

The solution to the second problem is, simply, the Mass. In each Mass a human being, lending his lips to his Lord, whispers: "This is my body." And with those awesome syllables he brings down on an altar the same Victim who died once for all on Calvary; he offers that same Victim to the Father for the sins of the world. In each Mass God gives us Calvary all over again. Not that He dies again; that He cannot do. But the Christ who rests on that altar is the same Christ, wounds and all, who died once for all on the cross.

The third problem. Once again we have two facts that clash. The first fact is the very nature of love. The dream of love is union—but perfect union, unending union, sensible and sensed, face to face and heart to heart. And, at the Supper, such was the disposition of the heart of Christ. "I have loved you with an everlasting love" (Jer 31:3). He wanted perfect, inseparable oneness with His own, with us—not only in spirit, not merely in poetry, but heart beating against heart.

That is the first fact, the dream of love, love's yearning for union. But, in conflict with the dream of love, we find the law of providence. This total self-giving is something reserved for heaven. A union between man and God that is perfect and unending—why, that *is* heaven, and providence will not permit even Jesus to put heaven on earth.

The problem, then, is this: how will love follow its natural bent, its yearning for union, without going counter to the law? How satisfy that yearning for a union He cannot yet give? The solution is shockingly simple. When He takes bread into His healing hands, He murmurs, not simply, "This is my body," but, "Take and eat" (Mt 26:26). So, too, for the wine. Not simply, "This is my blood," but, "Drink of this" (Mt 26:27). It is the realization of the remarkable promise made in Capharnaum: "Amen, amen, I say to you, unless you eat the flesh of the Son of Man, and drink His blood, you shall not have life in you. He who eats my flesh and drinks my blood has life everlasting, and I will raise him up on the last day. For my flesh is food indeed, and my blood is drink indeed. He who eats me, he shall live because of me" (Jn 6:54–56, 58).

The solution is Communion. Providence is obeyed, and love is satisfied. He gives Himself, but beneath a veil. He unites Himself to us, but without making Himself felt. The union is a passing thing, but it is real—and it can be a daily thing, if only you wish it. It is not heaven, but it is awfully close.

Three challenges to His love; three incredible responses. He had to go, and He wanted to stay; so, He went, and He stayed: the *Real Presence*. He would have preferred a daily death, and yet He could die but once; so, the Victim of Calvary returns to us each day, still our Victim, still our Sacrifice: the Sacrifice of the *Mass*. He wanted perfect union, and perfect union is impossible this side of heaven; so, He gave us the next best thing, *Communion*—His own heart next to our own beating hearts. Is it any wonder that the Christian cries with St. Thomas Aquinas:

"See, Lord, at thy service low lies here a heart
Lost, all lost in wonder at the God thou art."[2]

---

[2] St. Thomas Aquinas, *Adoro te*, translated by Gerard Manley Hopkins, *loc. cit.*

16. The Holy Eucharist: Sacrament of Oneness

ONE DAY, during the Second World War, a tremendous event took place over the face of the earth. That day Christ our Lord, hiding His godhead and His manhood under the appearance of bread, pillowed His head on the tongue of a child in Baltimore's Cathedral. The same day the same Christ slipped past bursting shells and past the lips of a Marine in the Marshalls. The same day the same Christ braved the beaches of Normandy to rest His brow beneath a British helmet. The same Christ made His home next to the throbbing heart of an Italian peasant-woman, and bent low to a bomb shelter in Berlin. The same Christ rode with the pilot in the cockpit of a Japanese Zero-fighter, and fed the brave on Burma Road. Even barbed wire could not keep the same Christ from lighting up a brown face on Bataan.

You see, the Eucharist is above all a sacrament of oneness: it makes men one with Christ, and it makes men one with one another in Christ. And there you have the twin ideas I shall lay before you this afternoon: the body of Christ makes each of you one body with Him, and the body of Christ makes you and me one body with each other.

When our Lord sat down with the apostles to His Last Supper, He had less than twenty-four hours to live. And He knew it. In less than twenty-four hours the mother who watched her Son open His eyes on life in a manger, would watch her Son close His eyes on life from a cross. And, with Jesus gone, the world would seem a lonely world—almost as lonely as before Bethlehem.

It was not that He would leave us orphans. Because of Calvary His Father was to be our Father, His mother our mother, His Holy Spirit our fire of love. Because of Calvary Father, Son, and Holy Spirit would make their home in our spotless souls. But Christ our Lord knew us better than we know ourselves. He knew that, weak as we are, human as we are, we are restless, dissatisfied, unless we can see and touch and taste. But we cannot yet see His Father; we cannot touch His mother; we cannot taste His Holy Spirit. We cannot sense the Blessed Trinity dwelling in our souls.

And so, with a power genuinely divine, and with a tenderness genuinely human, He gave us something to see, to touch, to taste. He gave us something that looks like bread, that feels like bread, that tastes like bread—and is not bread. For in that outward cloak of bread He clothed Himself. "Take and eat; this is my body" (Mt 26:26).

We can look upon the snow-white wafer cradled in priestly hands, and know by faith that we are looking upon the swaddling-clothes of God-made-man. We can touch the helpless Host, and feel that we are touching the hem of God's garment. We can taste the flavor of bread, and realize that not bread but God Himself is our food. "Unless you eat my flesh and drink my blood, you shall not have life in you" (cf. Jn 6:54).

Nineteen hundred years ago, on Calvary, God left us. Ever since, through the Sacrifice of the Mass, God gives us Calvary all over again. But this time He returns to us—His flesh for food, His blood as drink. Little wonder St. Thomas Aquinas could sing so rapturously to this hidden God:

"Godhead here in hiding, whom I do adore
Masked by these bare shadows, shape and nothing more:
See, Lord, at thy service low lies here a heart
Lost, all lost in wonder at the God thou art."[1]

But the remarkable thing about the Eucharist is this: the body of Christ was meant to achieve a oneness, a union, not merely between my God and myself, but between myself and my fellow men. Simply because the Christ of the Eucharist is always one and the same Christ. For the Lord who locks Himself in the tabernacle of your body is none other than the Lord who nourishes the child at home and the soldier overseas, the same Christ who feeds the Filipino, the Chinaman, and the Briton, the Italian, the German, and the Japanese. Christ is not divided; Christ is not multiplied. There is not one body for you, and another body for your neighbor. There is not one Christ who is your food, and another Christ who is the food of Koreans. There is one and the same body, one and the same Christ, for all.

Not only that. As St. Paul phrases it so beautifully: *"Because* the Bread is one, we, though many, are one body, all of us who partake of the one Bread"* (1 Cor 10:17). When you assimilate the food of the body, you change it into your own substance. That is not true of the cloistered Christ. When Christ gives Himself to you as food, you are transformed into Christ. In the words that Augustine of Hippo heard from on high: "I am the food of grown men: grow and you shall eat me. And you shall not change me into yourself as bodily food, but into me you shall be changed." So much so that you can cry out with St. Paul: "I live, no longer I, but Christ lives in me" (Gal 2:20). In the felicitous phrase of Pius XII: "If you have received worthily, you are what you have received."

---

[1] St. Thomas Aquinas, *Adoro te,* translated by Gerard Manley Hopkins, *loc. cit.*

But remember: there is not one Christ into whom you are transformed, and another Christ into whom your enemy is transformed. All partake of one food, and all become one body, and that body is Christ. "You are all one in Christ Jesus" (Gal 3:28). For "he who eats my flesh and drinks my blood abides in me, and I in him" (Jn 6:57). A breathtaking thought, isn't it? Black or white, American or Korean or Malayan, "you are all one in Christ Jesus." And those who refuse to receive Him? Just as they will not rest till they rest in Him, so He will not rest till He rests in them.

My dear friends: The sacrament of Christ's body is above all a sacrament of oneness, the oneness of all men in Christ Jesus—all men who eat His flesh and drink His blood. But the sublime symphony of this sacrament is in danger of being drowned out by hymns of hate. You are told very frankly that, if you think you can hate the sin and love the sinner, if you kill your enemy and insist you love him, you are a hypocrite. The only way to win a war is to hate every hostile heart with a bitter hatred born in the bowels of your heart.

The theory overlooks a tremendous trifle: that God formed all men from the same clay, that God took this clay to Himself to save it, that the night before He was crucified for this clay He changed wheat and wine into His body and blood and whispered to the ages: "Take and eat; this is my body. Drink of this, all of you; for this is my blood" (Mt 26:26–28). Be afraid to be more Christian than Christ. Be afraid to hate those whom Christ refuses to hate, because they are children of the same Father, because so many of them have tabernacled the Son of God within their fragile frame. Remember, above all, that this sacrament of oneness here below is but a foretaste and a pledge of that unending oneness with God and men which Thomas Aquinas hymned so masterfully:

"Jesu whom I look at shrouded here below,
I beseech thee send me what I thirst for so,
Some day to gaze on thee face to face in light
And be blest for ever with thy glory's sight."[2]

[2] St. Thomas Aquinas, *Adoro te,* translated by Gerard Manley Hopkins, *op. cit.,* p. 187.

17. ❦ The Crucifixion: God's Masterpiece of Love

THE INCIDENT took place in New York. It happened during the Second World War. It was evening; snow sparkled from the rooftops; and the gentleman I have in mind was walking down a darkened street. With him went his little boy. As they walked along, the youngster became very interested in the lighted windows of the houses. Interested, and a little puzzled. "Daddy," he asked, "why are there stars in some windows?" "Well, sonny," he was told, "a star in a window means: that house has given a son to the war." As they passed house after house, star upon star, the little lad would clap his hands and cry: "Look, Daddy, there's a house that's given a son. . . . And there's another. . . . There's one with two stars. . . . And, Daddy, there's a house with three!" At last they came to a break in the houses. Through the gap could be seen the evening star twinkling in the sky. The little fellow caught his breath: "Ooh, look, Daddy," he cried, "look! *God* must have given *His* Son—He has a star in His window!"

My dear friends: The youngster in that story glimpsed the tremendous truth that St. John expressed when he wrote: "God so loved the world that He gave His only Son" (Jn 3:16). Part of that tale of divine love is almost understandable. That God should have "pity on our childishness," that He should step down from heaven and put on not simply our dress but our flesh. There is beauty there, and poetry. We can almost understand how God could work with His hands, learn what hunger tastes like, have no place whereon to rest His head. There is still dignity there, and manhood. What is hard to understand is this: the Son of God was sold for silver, slapped and spat upon, whipped like a dog, and nailed to a tree. What is hard to understand is the Christ the prophet Isaias described centuries before the crucifixion:

"No form was His, no beauty, that we should gaze at Him;
    No comeliness, that we should desire Him.
Despised was He, and the réfuse of men,
    A man of sorrows. . . .

"He was pierced for our transgressions,
    He was bruised for our misdoings;
The penalty of our peace lay upon Him,
    And by His stripes there was healing for us."

(Is 53:2–3, 5)

Yes, God had decided that the union between man and God which had been ruptured in paradise would be re-established on Calvary, that basically divine love would recapture man's heart through crucifixion—not the crucifixion of man, but the crucifixion of God! "If I be lifted up, I will draw all men to myself" (Jn 12:32).

The crucifixion of the Son of God is a sad event—as every Calvary must sadden us. The human spirit in its passion for life has never found it easy to look on death. Even our Lord prayed: "Father, if it be possible, let this chalice pass from me" (Mt 26:39). And yet, the crucifixion of Christ is not, at bottom, a sorrowful thing. There is a joy in it that is not of this world, a joy that transmutes the sorrow. We know that kind of joy; we have seen it. We saw it in Dickens' *Tale of*

Two Cities, when Sidney Carton went to the guillotine for an innocent man, with peace in his eyes, and on his lips: "It is a far, far better thing that I do than I have ever done." We saw it in the four chaplains who gave their lifebelts to others and knelt arm-in-arm on a deck until the ocean covered them. We see it in a mother's supreme sorrow: that she cannot clutch to *her* breast the fever that burns her child, that she cannot exchange her life for a loved one's lifelessness. There is joy, there is ecstasy in the crucifixion, because this above all— more than the crib, more than the palm-branches—this above all is what the Son of God *wanted.* "There is a baptism," He said, "I must needs be baptized with, and how impatient, how oppressed am I until it be accomplished!" (Lk 12:50). It is love that redeems the sadness: "God so *loved* the world. . . ."

There is one thing harder still to understand. Christ our Lord was crucified not for a misty mass called humanity. He died for Adam, that strange creature who could not abide in God's love for the space of one temptation. He died for Judas as well as for John, for Mary of Magdala as well as Mary of Nazareth. He died for *both* thieves who were crucified with Him, even for the bandit who kept cursing Him. He died for *you,* as though Christ and His cross had arms only for you. In fact, each one of you is so precious in His eyes that, if you alone loved Him, if only you out of all creation bent your knee to Him, the crown of thorns would have been worth the pain. No wonder St. Paul never wearied of whispering: "He loved *me*—He gave Himself up for *me*" (Gal 2:20). Oh, of course it is unbelievable:

> "Strange, piteous, futile thing!
> Wherefore should any set thee love apart?
> . . . Thou knowest not
> How little worthy of any love thou art!

Whom wilt thou find to love ignoble thee
Save Me, save only Me?"[1]

It is so unbelievable as to be blasphemous, had we not God's own word for it. Why *me?* The answer is hidden in the mystery that is God. We do not know. But centuries before Calvary the chosen people, lonely in exile, cried out in anguish: "The Lord hath forsaken me, the Lord hath forgotten me!" Do you know what God's answer was? "Can a woman forget her infant, so as not to have pity on the son of her womb? And if she should forget, yet will not I forget thee" (Is 49:14–15). The crucifixion etches in tragedy what Christ never ceased to teach by word: God is a Father.

My dear friends: There is a problem in the crucifixion. But the problem does not lie with God. The crucifixion is God's masterpiece of love: to give until there is nothing left to give. That is why the words that wounded Christ most on the cross, the words that hurt His heart beyond all healing, were two simple words: "Come down. . . . Come down from the cross!" (Mk 15:30).

The problem lies rather with us. To a Christian—St. Paul tells us—"life is Christ" (Phil 1:21). To be a Christian is to reproduce Christ. Not only the sheer *joy* of human living when lived in union with God, but even more to relive in my own life the Man who was, above all else, a "man of *sorrows*." To give until there is nothing left to give. That is not to be morbid. Sorrow will come, increasingly as the years move on. No human heart escapes crucifixion. But the problem lies in this: crucifixion is a test, a test of love. There is a long road between Palm Sunday and Good Friday—and that road is the Way of the Cross. The same voices that shouted "Hosanna" on Sunday blasphemed Christ on Friday. It is all too easy to

[1] Francis Thompson, "The Hound of Heaven," ed. Wilfred Meynell, *loc. cit.*

love God, all too hard to prove your love, when the sky is serene. But let the dark clouds gather—let sickness come, poverty, the death of a dear one—let anything come that paralyzes your mind and puts a real physical ache in your heart—and you are tempted to cry out: "My God, why did you do *this* to me? Why did you let *this* happen? Anything else, Lord—but why *this*?" And only your grief keeps you from hearing the sweet words of Christ: "I did *this* to you because I love you. I let *this* happen because I want to see if you love me."

My dear friends: To one who loves, to one who loves God, the supreme insult, the most exquisite hurt, is the temptation: "Come down. . . . Come down from the cross!"

18. Come Down from the Cross!

DID YOU ever wonder what words wounded Christ most on the cross? Did you ever ask yourself what barb, what taunt, what bitter line hurt His heart beyond all else?

Before Calvary our Lord tasted much bitterness from the poisoned tongues of men. He canceled the sins of a paralytic, and the scribes said in their hearts: "He blasphemes" (Mk 2:7). He promised His flesh for food, and His disciples murmured: "This is a hard saying" (Jn 6:61). He cast a devil from a tortured soul, and the crowds cried: "He casts out devils by the prince of devils" (Lk 11:15). He opened the eyes of the blind, and the Pharisees insisted: "We know this man is a sinner" (Jn 9:24).

Blasphemer, devil, sinner: such was the endless echo of His life. Half a hundred times they tore at His heart with their tongues; and half a hundred times it did not seem so hard to take. Each biting word was a step to a cross, and the cross was the goal that shaped His human living. Why? Because, as He promised, "If I be lifted up from the earth, I will draw all men to myself—*if* I be lifted up" (Jn 12:32). To bring forth fruit, the grain of wheat had to "fall into the ground and die" (Jn 12:24).

On that cross everything hinged. A whole world would cease to hang over hell, only if Christ hung over Calvary. Just

as, in a rude chapel or a towering cathedral, all the lines con-
verge on one spot, the altar—so too every thought of our
Lord, every syllable, every gesture looked forward to the
cross. Peter learned that to his shame and sorrow. For, when
Jesus "began to show His disciples that He must go to Jerusalem, and suffer, and be put to death," Peter took Him aside:
"Never, Lord! No such thing shall befall thee." And Jesus
turned on Peter almost savagely: "Back, Satan! Thou art a
stone in my path; for these thoughts of thine are man's, not
God's" (Mt 16:21–23).

That is why the words that wounded Christ most in His
passion were not the bloodcurdling cry, "Crucify Him!" (Mk
15:13). The words that wounded Him worst were simple
words: "Come down! Come down from the cross!" (Mk
15:30). The priests and passers-by hurled the words at Him
in mockery: "If thou art the Son of God, come down from the
cross!" (Mt 27:39–44). The thief at His left whispered it in
agony: "If thou art the Christ, save thyself and us!" (Lk
23:39). The apostles framed the plea within their hearts, in
love: "Come down! There is still time, time to ask your Father
for twelve legions of angels, time to save yourself, time to
come down."

But, whether the words were framed in mockery, or in
agony, or in love, the effect was the same: they hurt—they
hurt the heart of Christ. No matter what the speakers meant
by it, the challenge to come down is a contradiction. It is an
invitation to forget the one thing that gives meaning to all that
has gone before; an invitation to abandon the work of redemption before He can say, "It is finished" (Jn 19:30); an invitation to cease being Saviour. Do you remember the temptation
in the desert, at the beginning of His public life? "If thou art
the Son of God, command that these stones become bread."
His answer? "It is not by bread alone that man lives" (Mt

4:3–4). The temptation at the end of His public life is more subtle still: "If thou art the Son of God, come down from the cross." His answer might well have been: "It is not by a *descent* from the cross that man will come alive." For, if anything is clear from the Gospel story, it is God's plan for man's redemption, the plan put so simply by St. Matthew: "Jesus began to show His disciples that He must go to Jerusalem, and suffer, and be put to death" (Mt 16:21). "*If* I be lifted up, I will draw all men to myself" (Jn 12:32). For God had decreed, once and for all, that the oneness between man and God which had been sundered in Eden would be restored on Calvary, that divine love would retake man's heart through crucifixion.

"Come down from the cross"? Why, Christ our Lord might well have whispered: "How blind you are! You don't understand, do you? I love you. I love you so intensely that I am not content to *live* for you; I want to die for you. Yes, I could have won your love with my *life*: I could have redeemed you in a manger, in the desert, in the waters of the Jordan, on a donkey's back. But I want to prove to you that there is no greater love than this, that *God* should lay down His life for His *enemies*. I want you to realize that love, be it man's or God's, is too blind to ask, 'How much do I have to do?' Love only asks, 'What more can I do?' "

The secret of the cross is love; and you cannot, you dare not, reason with love. For those who love, no explanation is necessary; for those who do not love, no explanation is possible. As St. Augustine phrased it so admirably: "Where there is love, there is no labor; and if there is labor, the labor is love."

My dear friends: What Christ our Lord has done for men out of love, men will do for Christ—out of love. You may remember how St. Andrew, Peter's brother, saw the cross prepared for his flesh, and cried from afar: "O sweet cross, graced by the limbs of my Lord, take me from men and give me back to my Master, that through thee He may receive me, who through thee redeemed me."[1] And, had you begged him, "Come down from the cross," Andrew would have answered: "You don't understand. Where there is love, there is no labor; and if there is labor, the labor is love."

You may remember St. Isaac Jogues. Here was a man who gave his life to savages in what is now New York State. A human being who ran the Indian gauntlet, and on the summit of the Hill of Torture took his severed thumb, placed it on the paten of his mangled hands, and offered it to God. A martyr who returned to his savages and found what he expected to find: a tomahawk for his skull. And, had you begged him, "Come down," Isaac would have answered: "Where there is love, there is no labor; and if there is labor, the labor is love."

Dear friends in Christ: Today, as every day, there is no one of you without your cross. It matters not what makes the cross: loneliness or lovelessness, poverty or pain, the thousand and one "tremendous trifles" that crucify the human frame. What does matter is the secret of the cross. The enemies of Christ, like the priests and the curious on Calvary, will always ask: "Isn't it foolish to stay on a cross when you can come down?" Those who are nailed to a cross against their will, like the thief on the left, will always ask: "Isn't it foolish to stay on a cross when you can save yourself and others?" And even the friends of Christ, like the apostles, still need the Holy Spirit before they realize that "the foolishness of God is wiser than men" (1 Cor 1:25). The secret of the cross is summed up in the words the priest speaks to every young couple about

---

1 *The Passion of Andrew* 10; edited by M. Bonnet, in R. Lipsius and M. Bonnet, *Acta apostolorum apocrypha* 2/1 (Leipzig: Mendelssohn, 1898), 25–26.

to join their hands and their hearts on the steps of an altar: "Sacrifice is usually difficult and irksome. Only love can make it easy, and perfect love can make it a joy."

Every cross is planted close to the cross of Christ. For either your cross is on His left hand, and you curse Christ for not taking you down—that is the wisdom of the world. Or your cross is on His right hand, and you whisper only, "Lord, remember me" (Lk 23:42)—that is "the foolishness of God."

To the temptation, "Come down from the cross," the Christian has but one answer: "You don't understand. Where there is love, there is no labor; and if there is labor, the labor is love."

19. Why This Waste?

FIVE DAYS before His death Christ our Lord came to Bethany. "And they made Him a supper there" (Jn 12:2). Lazarus, whom He had raised from the dead, was at table with Him. Martha served. And a woman called Mary took a pound of precious ointment, poured it on the feet of Jesus, and dried His feet with her hair. But the disciples were indignant and one of them murmured: "Why this waste? This might have been sold for much and given to the poor" (Mt 26:8–9; Jn 12:4–5).

Dear friends in Christ: That protest, "Why this waste?", has echoed down the centuries. Not for a pound of precious ointment, but for the precious blood of Christ. Not because Mary poured out perfume, but because the Son of God poured Himself out like wine. Why *this* waste? Why could not Christ have spared Himself the expense of the passion? Why could not Christ have poured on us a less costly ointment than His blood? Why could not Christ—God that He was—have thought of a cheaper redemption than Calvary?

The answer is simple: He *could* have. . . . Christ could have redeemed you in *Bethlehem*. That night God made a stable His heaven, a feeding trough His throne, surrounded Himself with animals for angels. Why, the cold night air purpling the baby lips was enough to redeem a thousand worlds—simply because the baby lips were the lips of God. Then, why this waste?

Christ could have redeemed you at *Nazareth*. There Jesus, who had made the world out of nothing, learned from Joseph how to turn out a plow. There Jesus, who was Himself the God of love, learned from Mary how to love God. Why, one trip to the well for water was enough to redeem a thousand worlds—simply because the boyish feet were the feet of God. Then, why this waste?

Christ could have redeemed you in the *desert*. There the sinless Christ fasted for forty days. There the devil tempted his God. There Satan said to our Saviour: "Command that these stones become bread" (Mt 4:3). Why, one pang of hunger was enough to redeem a thousand worlds—simply because the hunger was the hunger of God. Then, why this waste?

Christ could have redeemed you with a *word*—any one of the wondrous words of Christ: "Father, I will that where I am, they also whom thou hast given me may be with me" (Jn 17:24). "Forgive us, as we forgive" (Mt 6:12). "Be of good heart, son: thy sins are forgiven thee" (Mt 9:2). "Woman, hath no man condemned thee? Neither will I condemn thee" (Jn 8:10–11). Why, one breath from the mouth of Christ was enough to redeem a thousand worlds—simply because it was the breath of God. Then, why this waste?

Christ could have redeemed you when He rose from supper and like a slave, half-naked, washed the feet of Peter. He could have redeemed you with *one* lash on His back, *one* thorn in His brow, *one* slap of His cheek. Why, Christ could have redeemed a thousand worlds with the kiss of Judas. Then, why this waste?

Why was the soul of Christ "sorrowful even unto death" (Mt 26:38)? Why did the sweat of Christ become "as drops of blood trickling down upon the ground" (Lk 22:44)? Why was the cup of Christ so bitter that He asked His Father to remove it? Why was God mocked for a fool, beaten to a pulp, sentenced to death? Why did God hang on a cross for three hours with nails burning His flesh? Why did Christ die like the thieves between whom He was crucified?

I will tell you why: God planned our redemption *so that we could not mistake it.* . . .

We might have missed the meaning of *Christmas.* It is so simple to concentrate on the song and the star and the love-light in Mary's eyes—so easy to forget that Christmas has no meaning unless it means that the Child had pity on our childishness. We can forget that in Bethlehem forgiveness was born.

We might have missed the meaning of *Nazareth.* Even the Nazarenes saw too much of the boy in Jesus, too little of the God. You can dream at Nazareth; you cannot dream beneath a cross.

We might have missed the meaning of that first Lent—Lent in a *desert.* When the hungry Christ commands, "Begone, Satan!" (Mt 4:10), it is too easy to be thrilled with His triumph, too easy to forget that it is not Christ but the Christian who must carry heaven by violence.

We might have missed the meaning of His *words.* They fall too easily from our lips—like honey—like the Our Father that mounts so monotonously to heaven. "*Thy* will be done," and we do our own. "Forgive us, as we forgive," and we refuse to forgive.

But, agonize an hour with God in Gethsemane, pass a lonely night in His prison, see Pilate wash his hands of Him, hear Herod laugh at Him, bend over the pillar as leaden thongs tear His back, walk the Way of the Cross, kneel down on Calvary and catch the eyes closing in death—can you possibly mistake the meaning of *this*? Can you echo the despair of Cain: "It's not enough: *my* sins are too scarlet" (cf. Gn 4:13)? You might have said so in the stable, in His home, in the desert. You cannot say it on Calvary. Not unless you are blind, blind as the men who tore the heart of Christ by crying: "If you want us to believe, *come down*, come down from the cross!" (cf. Mt 27:42).

Why this waste? To open the eyes of even the blind, to touch the heart of a stone, so that like the centurion every human being will be forced to confess: "Truly this man was the Son of God" (Mk 15:39), and like the crowd you too will leave Calvary beating your breast and repeating with St. Paul: "He loved *me* and gave Himself up for *me*" (Gal 2:20). The extravagance of the crucifixion tells me more vividly than words what a vicious thing sin must be, if God was willing to nail sin in His own body to a tree. There never was a sin—yours or mine or anyone else's—there is no sin now, and there never will be a sin, that was not crucified with Christ, that did not crucify Christ.

Not only that. The lavishness of Christ's love is the measure of my real worth. At the foot of the cross, is self-pity still possible? Can I still mouth the beatitude that is not Christ's: "Blessed are you when men shall praise you and speak all that is good of you"? Whatever men may think of me, or may not think, I must be fearfully and wonderfully made if God went to such extremes of love to win me. "He loved *me* and gave Himself up for *me*."

More than that. With the passion, pain was made precious. My pain. The suffering that has racked bodies and tormented minds with an unanswerable "why" ever since Eden, finds meaning on Calvary. Very simply: life can be purchased by death. In God's wisdom, the way to God is through crucifixion. Pain, offered to God on the paten of my flesh, can be redemptive. My body need never be useless: the weaker it is, the stronger it is. Crucifixion, deliberately elected or patiently accepted for love of God or of God's images on earth, can win life, God's life, for me and for those I love.

Dear friends in Christ: If you are ever tempted to think the passion a waste, it may help to recall who it was first asked: "Why this waste?". . . It was *Judas*.

20. My God, My God, Why Hast Thou Forsaken Me?

This afternoon I am afraid I may hurt you. Because I want to say something about a very human thing. Something as human as love, because it is rooted in love. Something so human, there is hardly a heart without it.

If you are a mother or a father, you will know what I mean. If your day, busy as it is, has ever been filled with waiting, you will know what I mean. If the other half of your heart you have given to your country or back to God, you will know what I mean. If you have ever worn a uniform, be it a stone's throw from home or in the inferno of a foxhole, you will know what I mean. If you are a child with an ache in your heart, you will know what I mean. If you are old, and your friends are afar, and you are convinced, rightly or wrongly, that "nobody loves you," you will know what I mean. If you have ever lost God for even an hour, you will know what I mean. If you have ever cried your heart out, if you have ever tried to cry and could not, you will know what I mean.

Adam felt it, when he found himself outside paradise, without God: Adam was lonely. Eve felt it, when she rocked the body of Abel in her arms, unable to understand that for the first time life had gone out of a human being: Eve was lonely. Mary felt it, when she stood at her door and waved to her

Son as He turned the road, bound for souls and a cross at the end: Mary was lonely.

But, above all, above Adam and Eve and even Mary, Christ felt it: our Lord was lonely. He was born lonely, so lonely that an angel sent shepherd lads scurrying over the hillside to tell the Infant how much they loved him. He grew up lonely, in a rude village where everyone knew His every secret, save the one big secret, that Jesus was God. He lived lonely. He went about His Father's business, and even His mother did not quite understand. He "came unto His own, and His own did not welcome Him" (Jn 1:11). He promised His flesh for food, His blood as drink, and His own disciples "turned back and walked no more with Him" (Jn 6:67). He trained twelve apostles for three years, and on a single night one sold Him for silver, another denied Him with an oath, and to a third He could whisper with infinite sadness: "Have I been so long a time with you, and you have not known me?" (Jn 14:9).

But Christ our Lord was not only born lonely; He not only grew up lonely; He not only lived lonely. Christ our Lord died lonely. A loneliness that began in a garden, pressed on Him in a prison, and came to a climax on a cross.

It began in a garden. In the garden of Gethsemane, where the soul of Christ was "sorrowful even unto death," where the sweat of Christ "became as drops of blood trickling down upon the ground," where the cup of Christ was so bitter that He begged His Father to remove it,—our Lord looked for *one* to grieve with Him, and there was *none*: His disciples were sleeping for sorrow. He looked for *one* to comfort Him, and He found *one*: an angel from heaven, a messenger from the face of His Father. And, with the angel of the agony steadying His cup, He rose from the blood-red earth and went to meet His executioners.

That night the Son of God passed in a prison. Alone. The

high priest who charged Him with blasphemy, the elders who
spat in His face, the attendants who struck him, all were
asleep. Only Christ was sleepless, awake with His thoughts.
Lonely thoughts. Thoughts of Judas, who shared His heart:
Judas, who would hang himself with a halter. Thoughts of
Peter, head of His Church: Peter, who swore he had never
looked into the eyes of Christ. Thoughts of James and John,
who could not watch one hour with Him. Thoughts of Philip
and Andrew and all the rest, huddled together like little children afraid of the dark. Thoughts of Mary, whom He must
give away. . . .

But the loneliness of Christ came to a climax on the cross.
There the Son of God shattered the sky above Calvary with
a cry of unutterable loneliness: "My God, my God, why hast
thou forsaken me?" (Mt 27:46). To get some insight into
that dark outburst, you must lay hold of a paradox: on the
cross Christ our Lord was lonely—but He was not alone.

He was lonely—inexpressibly lonely. The words on His
lips—"why hast thou forsaken me?"—are the opening words
of what is, in the Hebrew, Psalm 22. That Psalm voices the
cry of a just man in profound desolation: God has "forsaken"
him in the sense that God has given him over to his enemies,
has let the wicked have their way with him. That abandon-
ment, that desolation of which the Psalmist sings, finds its fulfilment (Jesus tells us), it is realized, in Him, in the crucified
Christ. It is *His* passion, *His* loneliness that the Psalm portrays
when the just man goes on to say:

"I am a worm and not a man,
    A shame to mankind, and despised of the people.
    All who see me make sport of me;
    They make mouths at me and toss their heads.

"I am poured out like water,

And all my bones are disjointed.
My heart is like wax,
Melted in the midst of my bosom."
                                        (Ps 21 [= Hebrew 22] :7–8, 15)

Yes, Christ on the cross was lonely. But He was not alone.
Psalm 22—"why hast thou forsaken me?" (v. 2)—is a cry
of desolation, yes; but it is a testimony of tremendous trust
as well—unassailable confidence in God. The just man forsaken continues to say: *"My* God—*my* God." Given by God
to his enemies, he goes on to pray:

"In thee our fathers trusted;
    They trusted and thou didst deliver them.
    Unto thee they cried and were set free;
    In thee they trusted and were not disgraced."
                                        (vv. 5–6)

So, too, Christ our Lord. Surrounded His life long by forget-
fulness, surrendered in His last hours to wickedness, He had
always one consolation to fall back upon, one thing the world
could not take from Him—the secret solace He revealed when
He murmured: "I am not alone. The Father is with me" (Jn
8:16).

My dear friends: Loneliness, I am afraid, is a fact inseparable from human living. It is a sorrow that will be increasingly yours as the years go on, as God strips from you, one
by one, your very human loves, the attachments that are the
bitter-sweet of life on earth. The one genuine answer, the one
Christian answer, to the problem of loneliness is the secret of
Christ: to be lonely without ever being alone. But that involves, on your part, a twin realization.

You must realize, in the first place, that the loneliness of
our Lord was not an accidental thing, a sorrow He suffered

because He could not shun it. Like His hunger in the desert, like His weariness at the well, like His sweat of blood in the garden, His loneliness too was deliberately elected; it was part and parcel of His redemptive role. "We have not," St. Paul insisted, "a high priest who cannot have compassion on our infirmities, but one tried as we are in *all* things save sin" (Heb 4:15). He took to Himself *our* loneliness: the loneliness of every mother for the child of her womb, be he treacherous like Judas, repentant as Peter, warm as John; the loneliness of every child athirst for a glimpse of its father; the loneliness of a lover for a loved one; the loneliness of the friendless, the outcast, the aged; the loneliness of every Christian crucified between heaven and earth, unable to see God for the clouds, dear ones through tears. In the loneliness of Christ your loneliness was made precious, because your tears are mingled with the tears of God, the water with the wine, in the one chalice.

A second realization, just as important. Like the just man in Psalm 22, you too can say from the depths of dereliction: *"My* God." Simply because He never ceases to be *your* God. And like the Christ of Calvary, you too can always murmur: "I am not alone. The Father is with me." For, as someone phrased it with rare insight, He does not forsake us unless we first forsake Him. And even then the words of God to Israel in exile are true of us: "Can a woman forget her infant, so as not to have pity on the son of her womb? And if she should forget, yet will not I forget thee" (Is 49:15).

My dear friends: Loneliness is a test of your trust. If you are a human being, you must needs be lonely; if your eyes are fixed on God, you need never be alone.

21. Sacrifice: Suffering with a Purpose

Isn't it strange? Two convicts were crucified with Christ on Calvary; only one heard Him promise, "This day thou shalt be with me in paradise" (Lk 23:43). Isn't it pitiful? Two sinners suffered the selfsame agony; only one profited from his pain—the other cursed Christ for keeping him on his cross. Why? Because for one the cross was sheer suffering; for the other the cross meant sacrifice. But suffering and sacrifice are not one and the same thing; it is the tragedy of a bewildered world to have confused them. Sacrifice is suffering with a purpose. Let me explain.

I heard a story recently, a story hard to believe, a story all too true. It is the story of a young married couple—let us call them John and Mary. John and Mary had been married only a few short weeks when it happened: John was touched with creeping paralysis. Three months, and he was blind; six months, and he was stone deaf; one year, and he was paralyzed from the waist down.

Each morning Mary went out to work for John; each noon she came home to feed him; each afternoon she went back to work; each night she took care of him like a baby. Day in and day out, week after week, month after month.

One evening their closest friend came to dinner. One look at Mary was enough: "Mary," he said, "you've got to get out of here; you just can't go on like this; why, you've aged ten years in one." "Jim," she said, "you don't understand." "I do understand," he answered. "Oh, I know you married him for better or for worse. But not for this. Even God doesn't expect this of you. You're still young, still pretty; you have a whole life before you. And you're throwing it away. On what? Look at him! He can't see you; he can't hear you; he can't move. Why don't you get out while you still have a chance?"

Mary looked at Jim, hurt . . . hurt. "Jim," she said, "you don't understand. I love him. . . . I love him."

Sacrifice is suffering with a purpose. You see, the world has long since learned a lesson: that perfect oneness with an object beloved—be it man, woman, or child, be it music or medicine, knowledge or art—perfect oneness with an object beloved can be achieved only in terms of self-giving. It is the same truth that was chiseled in deathless lauguage by the Son of God when He said: "A woman about to give birth has sorrow, because her hour has come. But when she has brought forth her child, she no longer remembers the anguish for her *joy* that a man is born into the world" (Jn 16:21). Of course something is lost—in all sacrifice something is lost. But in the light of the gain the loss is no loss at all.

But in Christian suffering, in Christian self-denial, where is the gain? The gain is, simply, God . . . God. And in the light of the gain the loss is no loss at all. Again, let me explain.

God has no need of fasts. Why, then, does He ask them? God reaps no joy from cancer. Why, then, does He send it? Not because God is what He is, but because I am what I am. The more of self there is in me, the less room there is for God. The more I do my own will, the less I do His. There is but one basic reason why a man does not love God: he loves himself. There is but one reason why a man is not caught up in his Creator: he is wrapped up in himself. And so, because I want to love God more than myself, I deny myself some of the sweet nothings my nature craves—the sleep, the smoke, the meat, the drink. Because I want to make room for God, I take the headache and the heartache, pain of body and pain of soul, in the spirit of Job: "The Lord has given, and the Lord has taken away: blessed be the name of the Lord" (Jb 1:21). In suffering and self-denial, what I give is real, sometimes terribly real; that is why it hurts. But that gift must be symbolic—symbolic of something still more real: the gift of myself. For unless the gift, unless the suffering goes not merely out, but *up*, it profits me nothing.

To be transformed into sacrifice, suffering must be born of love—or, at least, suffering must end in love. Which, for a Christian, is the same as to say: suffering must begin with God, and suffering must end in God. Suffering must be born of love. For, as St. Paul tells us in that magnificent outburst: "If I distribute all my goods to feed the poor, and if I deliver my body to be burned, and have not charity—[if I do not love God]—it profits me nothing" (1 Cor 13:3). And suffering must end in love, must end in God. For, as St. Paul tells us again, in strong language inspired by God: "The things that were gain to me, the same, for the sake of Christ, I have counted loss. For His sake I have suffered the loss of all things, and I count them as dung that I may gain Christ" (Phil 3:7–8).

Quite some years ago there was a motion picture called *Claudia.* The character who plays the title role is a gay, carefree, utterly unsophisticated, supremely happy young wife. But Claudia has just been told that her mother, the mother she loves so deeply, the mother on whom she depends so frightfully, is about to die. Pain sears Claudia's breast like a cancer. And David, her husband, murmurs to the pain-crazed girl: "Make friends with pain, Claudia, and it'll stop hurting you." A lovely thought: "Make friends with pain, and it'll stop hurting you." A lovely thought, but not quite true. Pain, as long as it remains pain, will never quite stop hurting. The solution is more profound: "Make friends with God—make friends with God, and there will be a purpose to pain."

It is love that turns suffering into sacrifice. And it is love of God that gives a deep purpose to pain: love of God for what He is in Himself, love of men as the images of God. If you kneel long enough at the feet of the Crucified, you who labor and are heavy-burdened will begin to see why, as Francis Thompson put it, "nothing begins and nothing ends, that is not paid with moan," why "we are born in others' pain, and perish in our own."[1] You will begin to understand what Francis of Assisi meant when he said: "It is in giving that we receive; it is in loving that we are loved; it is in dying that we are born to eternal life." You will understand it if you understand the deeper meaning of the little story with which I shall end.

In a Paris garret there lived an artist. Starving, shivering, sleepless—but he had an idea, a dream, a vision—a vision that simply had to be incarnated in clay. And so he slaved, day after day, night after night, till the vision was captured in his clay. And one night—still starving, still shivering, still sleepless—he stood off and looked in reverence at his masterpiece. But at that moment, through the broken skylight, a single snowflake fell, caressed his cheek. And he knew, with a stab of fear, that the cold would crack his clay. So he took off his coat, his one warm covering, and wrapped it round his creation. When the cold dawn broke, the artist lay dead—but his love was alive!

---

[1] Francis Thompson, "Daisy," ed. Wilfred Meynell, *op. cit.*, p. 5.

The Resurrection and the
Resurrectional Life

22. The Significance of Easter

ON HOLY THURSDAY we sat in on the Last Supper, and our hearts leaped as we watched wheat and wine change for the first time into the body and blood of Christ. On Good Friday we stood beneath a cross, and our hearts sank as we watched the body of Christ waste away like chaff, watched His blood pour out like wine. On Easter Sunday we knelt before an open tomb, and our hearts took wing once more, because an angel told us that the body and blood of Christ were not there: "He has risen; He is not here" (Mk 16:6).

But, is that all there is to Holy Week? Are Holy Thursday, Good Friday, and Easter Sunday nothing but three tremendous days: on Thursday we were stunned by the goodness of God, on Friday we were grieved at the malice of men, on Sunday we were glad once again because God and goodness had risen from the grave? It that all there is to Holy Week?

My dear friends: Holy Week is like the seamless robe of Christ. Holy Thursday, Good Friday, and Easter Sunday are a coat of many colors, yes; but the coat is all of one piece. And the piece that links the crucifixion on Calvary to the Supper in the Cenacle, the piece that links the resurrection to both the crucifixion and the Supper, is summed up in one word: sacrifice—sacrifice for sin. Let me explain.

What is a sacrifice? Oh, not in the pocketbook, soap-opera, everyday sense of the word, but technically, as the theologian uses it, as it has been used by man before his God since the sacrifice of Cain and Abel. In the first place, I must *offer* something to God. I take something of my own, something that belongs to me, something I can see, and I give that, I offer that to God as a sign—a sign of something I cannot see: the gift, the offering to God of my own soul, my own will, my inmost being. That is why Cain, a husbandman, "offered, of the fruits of the earth, gifts to the Lord"; that is why Abel, a shepherd, "offered of the firstlings of his flock, and of their fat" (Gn 4:3–4). That something I can see, stands for me. By my offering I confess that I myself come from God, I depend on God, I am going to God. By my offering I confess that I am God's.

But with the entrance of sin on the human scene, something has been added. Sacrifice for sin calls for something more—something more than sheer offering. You see, sin is an offense against God's infinite majesty; if justice were done, the sinner would die. But God will not kill the sinner; and God's law forbids the sinner to kill himself. What, then, will he do? The Jews of old found an answer. They took an animal, say a spotless lamb, laid it on an altar, and slew it. Why? As a sign. Not that the lamb deserved to die. As a sign that they themselves deserved to die for their sins. Sacrifice calls for an offering; sacrifice for sin calls for a *victim*.

But a sacrifice is an offering made to *God*. It is up to God, then, to accept man's sacrifice or to reject it. You remember the words of Genesis: "The Lord took notice of Abel and his offering; but of Cain and his offering He took no notice" (Gn 4:4–5). And if God takes no notice, if God does not *accept* man's offering, man's sacrifice is useless. He can stand at an altar each dawning day, he may pour out the blood of unnumbered lambs, and in that blood concentrate the consecration of his whole soul, but if God frowns upon his offering, if God scorns his victim, the sacrifice is in vain and sinful man abides in his sin.

To have a sacrifice for sin, I must have three things: I must offer to God something of my own; that something must be slain; and God must accept my offering. Briefly, man must offer to God a victim that is welcome.

When the Son of God took flesh of Mary, He did so for a purpose. He took flesh to make satisfaction to God the Father for sin: for the sin that Adam passed on to you and to me and to every human being born into this world; for each and every sin that you and I and any man from Adam to Antichrist might ever commit. This satisfaction He intended to make in one way, and that way was . . . sacrifice, sacrifice for sin. And this particular sacrifice would be like any sacrifice for sin. Christ our Lord would offer God the Father something of His own; that something would be slain; and the fruit of His sacrifice, its power to satisfy for sin, would depend on God's acceptance. Briefly, Christ our Lord would offer the Father a victim that was welcome.

My dear friends: On Holy Thursday Christ our Lord *offered* to God the Father His gift for the sins of the world. On Good Friday that gift was *slain*. On Easter Sunday God the Father showed that He *accepted* the gift of His Son.

On Holy Thursday, when Christ took bread into His spotless hands, He did not simply say: "This is my body." He added something: "This is my body, which shall be delivered [to death] for you." When He took wine into His hands, He did not simply say: "This is my blood." He added something: "This is my blood, which shall be shed for you and for the multitude [of souls] unto the remission of sins" (Lk 22:19; Mt 26:28). At the Last Supper the gift was offered.

On Good Friday, because Christ so willed it, His enemies

took the body that had been offered for sin and bathed it with the blood that had been offered for sin. On the cross you have a Victim. On Calvary the gift was slain.

But, between Good Friday and Easter Sunday, a tremendous question mark hung suspended between heaven and earth: would God the Father accept the sacrifice of His Son? He did not have to. After all, it was not sinful man who was praying, "Forgive us our trespasses." It was the sinless God-man who had whispered, "Father, forgive them." If the Father said "No," if the Father insisted: "I do not want someone else's sacrifice; I want sinful man to do the impossible, I want finite man to make reparation for an infinite offense," then sinful man would still be in his sin. But on Easter Sunday God the Father showed His good pleasure in the sacrifice of His Son: He took the body that had been offered on Thursday, the body that had been slain on Friday, and He raised it from the dead. The gift had reached its goal: the body and blood of Christ, price of our forgiveness, was held in the hand of God forever. On Easter Sunday you have the sign of God's acceptance, the assurance that the Victim was welcome.

My dear friends: Should anyone ask you what Easter Sunday means to you, your answer is rather simple. Easter Sunday is that day on which we are assured that the sacrificial gift *offered* by Christ our Lord on Holy Thursday, the gift *slain* by His enemies on Good Friday, was *accepted* by God the Father for the sins of the world. Is it any wonder that on Easter we are supremely happy?

23. I Have Risen, and Am Still with You

QUITE SOME time ago I walked through a cemetery. It was not a Christian cemetery, but I shall never forget its name. A very consoling name, a name that reminded you of Calvary. It was called Hills of Eternity. I walked through path after path, past stone upon stone, by carpets of grass—each lovely plot an eternal hill. Suddenly I stopped, in surprise, before a massive memorial. I stopped because here alone the grass grew high; here alone the weeds were wild; here alone the stone itself seemed gray and cold. I looked closer. It was the grave of a young lad: only eighteen summers had been his. And beneath his name a single line was carved. I read the words, six short words, and I understood why the grass grew high, why the weeds were wild, why the wind seemed to sob as it fled past the stone. The inscription read: *How many hopes lie buried here!*

Nineteen hundred years ago that same inscription—six short words that etch a tragedy, six words that spell despair —that same inscription was graven on the grave of Christ. It was graven there by two disciples as they left Jerusalem after the burial of their Lord: "We had hoped that He was to be the Saviour of Israel" (Lk 24:21). It was graven there by eleven apostles huddled together in an upper room like little children afraid of the dark: "We had hoped." It was graven

there by Mary Magdalen as she watched Joseph roll a stone
to the door of the tomb, and she stood outside weeping: "We
had hoped." But how many hopes lie buried here!

And yet, forty short hours after hope had been buried the
same Christ stood before Magdalen: "Mary!" And she turned:
"Master!" (Jn 20:16). Perhaps eight hours more, and the
same Christ sat down to eat with Cleophas and his friend:
"and they recognized Him when He broke bread" (Lk
24:35). Six hours later, and the same Christ—the same Christ
who passed through the chaste cloister of Mary's womb, the
same Christ who passed through the sealed door of the tomb
—passed through the closed door of the supper room: "Peace
be to you!" And "He showed them His hands and His side"
(Jn 20:19–20).

My dear friends: With the resurrection of Christ death
could never be the same again, because life would never be
the same again. You remember the triumphal cry sounded by
the choir as the Easter Mass opens—the triumphal cry
snatched by the Church from the Psalms and touched to the
tongue of Christ: "I have risen, and am still with you." But
that cry is a cry of triumph not so much for Christ as for us
—not so much for God's Son who became man, as for man
who becomes God's son. Christ rose for the same reason that
He died: for us. That reason the Son of God put into words
the night before His death—perhaps the most thrilling sentence in the Gospel, the promise that has transformed human
life: "I live, and you shall live" (Jn 14:19).

Where is that life? It is here, and it is hereafter. No sooner
are you born than you are reborn. Water is poured upon you,
the Holy Spirit is poured out upon you, and a new life is
yours: the power to know and love God as God knows and
loves Himself. You are transformed into the likeness of your
risen Lord, a new creature, all alive with the life of God's

only Son. "I have risen, and am still with you." Better still:
"I have risen, and am *within* you." You grow up, and a bishop
oils your brow—in the shape, significantly, of a cross—for he
pours power into you to live that life courageously, to love
God even unto crucifixion. If you lose that life, even for
a moment, the risen Christ will restore it: "I'm sorry,
Lord. . . ." "And I, my child, I forgive you. *You* have risen,
and I am still with *you*." If you care to feed that life—"give
us this day our daily bread"—the risen Christ gives you Himself, the Bread of Life, for "unless you eat my flesh and drink
my blood, you shall not have life in you" (Jn 6:54). To pass
that life on to another generation, that Christ may say to
another age: "I have risen, and am still with you," you kneel
hand in hand at an altar, and husband gives to wife, wife
gives to husband, the wedding gift of grace, a little more of
God's own life. And as the shadows lengthen, and evening
comes, and the busy world is hushed, and the fever of life is
over, and your work is done, priestly hands—hands anointed
to bring life to men and men to life—anoint the senses which
have imperiled that life, to make easy and straight your passage, not from life to death, but from life with God on earth
to life with God in heaven.

Life with God in heaven. Of that resurrection our Lord's
resurrection is the model and the pledge. That is why I make
bold to put to you the question St. Paul flung at the Christians
of Corinth: "If Christ is preached as raised from the dead,
how do some of you say that there is no resurrection from
the dead?" (1 Cor 15:12). And, I insist, some of us do say
there is no resurrection from the dead. We say it in our pagan
flight from death, at every hopeless wake, though our Mother
the Church reminds us in each Mass for a dear Christian departed: "For those who believe, life is not taken away, life
is merely changed." We say it by our feverish absorption in

the things of earth, though St. Paul chides us: "If you be risen with Christ, seek the things that are above" (Col 3:1). We say it in our total attitude towards life: for so many of us, life begins at birth, or life begins at forty, but life never begins at death.

My dear friends: Ever since Calvary countless new stones have been rolled to countless fresh tombs. In our own sad memory all too many white crosses have risen over all too many grass plots. For each of us, somewhere in the wide world, there is a bit of earth that spells Calvary. But on all too many of those tombs we have graven the inscription of despair: How many hopes lie buried here! In a Christian grave one hope, and one hope alone, lies buried: the hope of a glorious resurrection after the manner of Christ's own rising. For, as St. Paul saw with rare insight, "if with this life only in view we have had hope in Christ, we are of all men the most to be pitied" (1 Cor 15:19). The cross on our dear graves is not a call to despair: "All hope abandon, ye who enter here."[1] The cross is a pledge that the life won for us by Christ, the life given us in baptism, the life kept aflame in us through the bitter-sweet of earthly living, will not die with death. It is a pledge that one day every tomb, like the tomb of Christ, will be empty. One day from every grave, from the ends of the earth and the bottomless sea, a dead body will rise to life, will join once more a soul that never died, and the risen Christian will face the risen Christ forever.

The resurrection of Christ—"I have risen, and am still with you"—is the promise of our own resurrection: the eternal day when each of us who lives the resurrectional life here below, each of us who believes and hopes and loves, will say to Christ: "I have risen, and am still with *you!*"

---

[1] Dante, *Divina commedia: Inferno*, Canto 3.

24. The Secret of Christian Joy

A PROVOCATIVE French novelist has put on the lips of one of his characters a stinging challenge: "You say you are a Christian. Then where the devil is your joy?" There, for many a pagan, is the real Christian scandal. He does not demand that we be heroes, simply because we are Christians. He may not even expect us to be good. But he does expect us to be happy.

The pity of it is that the pagan is right: so many of us are not happy. He has a right to wonder where that joy is which Christ said "no man shall take from you" (Jn 16:22). He has a right to be cynical when he contrasts with our joylessness St. Paul's "Rejoice always! I say to you, rejoice!" (Phil 4:4). He has a right to sneer if he sees that our joys are just the same as his, and therefore ultimately just as brief, just as bitter. I am afraid we have impressed the pagan with one-half of one beatitude: "Blessed are they that mourn" (Mt 5:5). Blessed are the melancholy.

May I recapture for you this afternoon the thrilling secret of Christian joy? I shall do that by emphasizing three points: (1) joy is a quality of *living*; joy flows from *life*; (2) for a Christian, joy flows from *eternal* life, from life without end; (3) this life without end has its beginning *now*.

First, then: joy is a quality of living; joy flows from life. You see, for something that lives, the supreme sorrow is death.

[137]

Death and all the lesser forms of death: pain, loss, lovelessness, loneliness. For death means the end. That is why even
the gentle deer, by sheer instinct, will fight savagely for its
life. That is why the tulip folds its chaliced petals at night to
protect the golden seed of life against the frost that would
blight it. That is why the last thing man clings to is life; even
when he has nothing to live for, he lives for life.

And the more life there is in us, the more joy. That is true
even on a sheerly natural level. You know the feeling of joy
that goes with physical well-being—when you feel so brimful
of life that it almost hurts. You know the joy there is in
mental activity, in mental achievement—the artist at his easel,
the scholar at his books, the man who thrills to his job—your
mind is alive, and that very living is joy. Above all, when you
are in love, you are alive—doubly alive, because someone
else's life has been fused with your own—you are living not
only your own life, you are living his. The more life there is
in you, the more joy.

God knows that. And there we have the meaning of His
message to men, the lesson God came on earth to teach. God
did not become man to teach us that we will suffer and die;
that much we could have learned for ourselves. God came on
earth to tell us that we will live. To tell us that death is not
an end, but a beginning. And not merely to tell us. He could
have told us through angels or prophets; He could have written it, like the ten commandments, on tablets of stone. No,
God proved it. God lived it. He died, but He rose to life
again. From that thrilling moment human life could never be
the same again, because death would never be the same again.
To me, the most joyous words in the Gospel are the few short
words the Son of God spoke to His disciples the night before
He was crucified, the promise of Christ that has transformed
human life: *"I live, and you shall live"* (Jn 14:19).

That is what we mean by eternal life. You who die in the arms of Christ will be alive as you have never lived before—doubly alive, because you will share God's own life, God's own love. Not for a precious hour to be stolen and then treasured in memory, but forever, days without end. Not in dribs and drabs, but as much as you are capable of absorbing, as much as your own heart's love can contain. Not merely in your soul, but reflected in your body as well—the same body as now, but without the pain, without the tears. Not to the destruction of your human affections: your joy will be increased by the presence of those you loved on earth, even as our Lord's affection for His mother led Him to want her with Him in heaven, even in her bodily frame.

Little wonder that Scripture, God's own handwriting, ends with St. John's cry of longing: "Come, Lord Jesus . . . come!" (Ap 22:20). For, as St. Paul remarked with such penetration: "If with this life only in view we have had hope in Christ, we are of all men the most to be pitied" (1 Cor 15:19). Each Mass for a dear Christian departed sounds the selfsame note of Christian joy: "For those who believe, Lord, life is not taken away; life is merely changed." Do you believe that? That death is not the end of life, but its beginning? That life begins not at birth, not even at forty, but at death?

And yet, even that is not quite true. Christian life, therefore Christian joy, does not *begin* at death. The remarkable aspect of eternal life, of eternal joy, is that it is not simply reserved for the other side of the grave. It has its beginning now. "If any man love me," the Son of God declared, "my Father will love him, and we will come to him and make our home with him" (Jn 14:23). We have God's own word for it that, if we love Him, He lives in us—we share His life—now. That is not just a bold metaphor. In sinlessness we bear heaven within us. True, heaven hides itself from our eyes.

God is not yet for us, as He was for St. John, "that which we have heard, that which we have seen with our eyes, have looked upon, and our hands have handled" (1 Jn 1:1). But we believe, on God's word, that within us rests God Himself.

There is the joy "no man can take from you"—no man except yourself. The realization that God, who *is* Love, loves you and in some mysterious way lives in you. That realization does not destroy natural joy. If you are one of those lovable individuals who are naturally gay and lightsome, God's love gives a lilt to your laughter, for it puts a rich meaning behind it, even adds an outward aura of serenity which is perhaps our most powerful argument for the faith that is in us. If your life is a tissue of sorrow, even in your anguish—as a perceptive writer phrased it—you will be "conscious of that lift of the heart which made one of the saints declare that joy was the inmost core of sorrow." It is only because of God's indwelling that you can be alone without ever being lonely.

Eugene O'Neill once wrote a play—a muddled play in many ways, but a play with a brilliant insight. It dealt with the life of Lazarus after the Son of God summoned him from the grave. O'Neill called his play *Lazarus Laughed*. It is the story of a lover of Christ who has tasted death and sees it for what it is. The story of a man whose one invitation to men is his constant refrain:

> "Laugh with me!
> Death is dead!
> Fear is no more!
> There is only life!
> There is only laughter!"

And O'Neill tells us: Lazarus "begins to laugh, softly at first," then full-throated—"a laugh so full of a complete acceptance of life, a profound assertion of joy in living, so devoid of all

. . . fear, that it is . . . infectious with love," so infectious that, despite themselves, his listeners are caught by it and carried away.[1]

And that, I submit, is Christianity. It is not that the Christian blinds himself to sin and war and disease and death. These touch him as cruelly as they touch the pagan. And still he can laugh, as the pagan can never laugh; still there is a joy in his heart which no man can take from him. For in the midst of death he has discovered life; for him, as for St. Paul, "life is Christ" (Phil 1:21).

---

[1] Eugene O'Neill, *Lazarus Laughed*, Act 1, Scene 1; in *The Plays of Eugene O'Neill* (New York: Random House, 1955), pp. 279-80.

25. Shrines of the Holy Spirit

Down through the ages God has come awfully close to us. To begin with, He fashioned this earth and sea and sky, and in fashioning them He painted His features on the canvas of the world. In a whirlwind there is something of God's power, a mountain mirrors His majesty, surging waves His irresistibleness, a star-flecked sky His breathtaking loveliness.

He came even closer to us when He took our flesh and walked with us, when a smile parted His lips and a tear fell from His eyes, when He ate and slept and fished and grew angry and loved and suffered and died in a forgotten corner of His world.

He came still closer when He left this world without quite leaving it. I mean, when He changed wheat and wine into His flesh and blood—when He stole into our bodies, His heart next to our own beating hearts—when for a precious quarter-hour the body and blood of God-made-man lingers lovingly within our own bodies.

But God knew that all this was not quite enough. Even when we "see His blood upon the rose, and in the stars the glory of His eyes,"[1] He is still too far from us. Even though

1 Joseph Mary Plunkett, "I See His Blood upon the Rose," in *The Catholic Anthology: the World's Great Catholic Poetry*, ed. Thomas Walsh (rev. ed.; New York: Macmillan, 1947), p. 428.

His footsteps did haunt the roads of Jerusalem, that was all so long ago. And though He pillows His head on our trembling tongues in Communion and nestles within our sorry frame, those fifteen minutes are a fleeting thing.

And so, the night before He died, the night He gave His flesh for food and His blood as drink, the Son of God made a remarkable promise. He knew His disciples were sorrow-laden because He was to leave them. And so He said to them, and through them to us: "I will ask the Father, and He will give you another to befriend you, one who is to dwell continually with you forever. It is the truth-giving Spirit, for whom the world can find no room, because it cannot see Him, cannot recognize Him. But you are to recognize Him; He will be continually at your side; in fact, He will be in you" (Jn 14:16–17).

"He will be in you." So, then, you need not search for God's face in the rainbow. You need not envy the people of Jerusalem who met their God in the streets. You need not pine away if the God who is your Communion flees from your body so soon. God is *in* you. That is the lesson of Pentecost. As long as you love God, God loves you, God lives in you. That is not pretty poetry, sheer metaphor. In sinlessness you bear heaven within you, as truly (though in a different way) as Mary for nine months bore beneath her heart her own little bit of heaven. We have God's word for it; and we have the thrilling echo of St. Paul: "Surely you know that your bodies are the shrines of the Holy Spirit, who dwells in you. And He is God's gift to you" (1 Cor 6:19).

But what does the Holy Spirit *do* within you? In the first place, it is a tremendous thing that He is there. Because He is there, you are a different person. You are a new creature, you are a child of God. The same Holy Spirit who graced the human frame of Christ our Lord, the same Holy Spirit who graces the glorified body of Christ at this moment in heaven, graces your soul. That is why, in the eyes of God, you are a lovely, lovable thing. In its sinlessness, in its love, your soul bears a striking resemblance to Christ. You are by grace, by gift, what He is by nature: you are sons and daughters of God.

And because the Holy Spirit is there, God the Father and God the Son are there as well. Remember the striking words of Christ: "If anyone love me . . . my Father will love him, and we will come to him and make our home with him" (Jn 14:23). Because He is there, you are a holy thing. The life of God flows within you, like another bloodstream. You are, as St. Paul insisted, shrines—you are temples.

But what does the Holy Spirit *do* within you? Do you remember the sign of the cross you made a few short moments ago? The Holy Spirit inspired that. Did it take some effort to make Mass this morning? The Holy Spirit brought you there. Did you receive God within your body at Holy Communion? The Holy Spirit prompted you. Each time you whisper, "I believe in God," each time you whisper, "My hope is in the Lord," each time you whisper, "I love you, God, above all things," the Holy Spirit is in that whisper. Each time you strike your breast, "Forgive me," the Holy Spirit moves your hand and your lips and your heart.

Briefly, He forms in your heart the beginning of every good thought, the beginning of every good desire, the beginning of every good action. From the first act of faith, through every act of hope, to your last act of love in life, it is the Holy Spirit who inspires it all. What does He do within you? Why, there is nothing good in you that He does *not* do!

If you want to see what the Holy Spirit *can* do, look at the apostles on the first Pentecost. At one moment, a handful of ordinary workingmen, hiding behind locked doors for fear of the Jews. The next moment they have flung themselves into the heart of Jerusalem; they preach Christ crucified to the people who crucified Him; each takes a section of the world for his mission, transforms it in the image of Christ, and dies a martyr's death. Why? Because something new has been added: the Holy Spirit as the moving force of their lives.

It is a tremendous thing, this gift of God to you. The same Holy Spirit who brooded over the waters when God made heaven and earth, the same Holy Spirit who spoke through the Old Testament prophets like Isaias and Jeremias, the same Holy Spirit who overshadowed a wisp of a girl and made her Virgin Mother of God, the same Holy Spirit who descended upon the apostles in tongues of fire and transformed cowards into heroes, the same Holy Spirit who is the soul of the Church and who keeps the Church holy and free of error, that is the Holy Spirit who dwells within you.

Yes, He can transform your lives, this Holy Spirit, if you will only let Him. And part of that transformation is something we rarely realize. Do you remember the words of Christ: "Peace I leave with you, my peace I give to you. Not as the world gives do I give to you" (Jn 14:27)? This is your peace, this gift of God to you, this Holy Spirit: the realization that in sinlessness you bear heaven within you, the realization that, if you love God, God loves you, God lives in you. There you have the peace no man can take from you—no man save yourself. Only one thing can destroy this peace, and that is . . . sin. Only one thing can preserve this peace, and that is . . . love.

Our Blessed Lady

26. The Abiding Meaning of Mary

WHEN THE mid-century Catholic thinks on the mother of Christ, there are three gifts of God to Mary that are quite vividly before him. There is, to begin with, God's first gift to Mary—we call it her *Immaculate Conception*. The Immaculate Conception simply means that, at the very first moment when God infused a human soul into the body that had been fashioned of Joachim and Anne, that soul thrilled to the divine life within it. To hold God within her, Mary did not have to wait for a baptism. At the very first moment there was a Mary, an angel could have said to her even then: "Hail, full of grace, the Lord is with thee, blessed art thou among women!" (Lk 1:28).

Secondly, there is the gift of God to Mary for which the Immaculate Conception was purely a preparation, the gift we honor each Christmas: Mary's *Virginal Motherhood*—the midnight in a stable when Mary looked upon her God and whispered: "This is *my* body."

Finally, there is the gift of God to Mary which the whole Catholic Church has recently honored: her *Assumption* to heaven in soul and body. As St. John Damascene said so beautifully twelve hundred years ago: "Just as the holy and incorrupt body that had been born of her rose from the tomb on the third day, so was it necessary that she too be snatched

[149]

from the grave and the mother restored to her Son. As He had descended to her, so was she carried up to Him."[1]

Around these three—Mary's Immaculate Conception, her Virginal Motherhood, her Glorious Assumption—the devotion of centuries has centered. This is the Mary the Church knows best. This is the Mary the Church proposes as the ideal of womanhood—in fact, all that is nearest and dearest to God in humankind.

And yet, precisely here we come face to face with a delicate problem. The problem lies in this: what is most characteristic of our Lady is inimitable. What makes Mary Mary, we cannot imitate. There is no one of you whose soul was graced with God's supernatural presence from the very first instant that you, a tiny bit of humanity, lay within your mother's womb. Mary's soul was. . . . There is no child of Eve, however dear to God, who is able to combine in her own person perpetual virginity and physical motherhood. Mary did. . . . There is no one of us whose body will escape the corruption of the grave, no one of us whose body will rejoin its soul before the glorious resurrection at the end of time. Mary's body did. . . .

Understand me. I do not say that Mary's sinlessness, Mary's humility before God's angel, Mary's courage in the face of her Son's crucifixion, should not be an inspiration to us. It should. What I do say is: Mary's most precious privileges, what makes Mary the unique creature she is—her Immaculate Conception, her Virginal Motherhood, her Glorious Assumption—are beyond our imitation. What, then, is their deep significance, their abiding meaning, for your life and mine? I will answer that question in several stages.

The first stage. Our Lady is a living lesson—God's fairest

---

[1] St. John Damascene, *Homily 2 on the Falling Asleep of Mary* 14 (*Patrologia graeca* 96, 741).

lesson next to her Son—our Lady is a living lesson in the meaning of holiness. Every one of her privileges—from her Immaculate Conception through her Virginal Motherhood to her Glorious Assumption—every one of her privileges is a living illustration of what holiness really is. And what is that? Holiness is simply . . . union with God. Why was that spotless embryo within the womb of Anne a holy thing, in fact the holiest thing on God's earth? Because God dwelt within it. Why was that teen-age virgin of Nazareth called by an angel "blessed among women"? Because the Son of God was to rest within her. Why is Mary supremely holy at this moment? Because, soul *and* body, she is one with God forever.

That much of the lesson is clear from our Lady's life: holiness is union with God. Let us go one step further. Union with God depends on two factors: on God and on man— on God's initiative and man's response. All holiness, all union with God, starts with God. It was God who kept sin from Mary's soul from the first moment of her existence. It was God who chose Mary to be the virgin-mother of His Son. It was God who lifted Mary, body and soul, to unending union with Him. All union with God starts with God.

But God always asks one question: "Will you?" That is why He asked Mary: "Will you be the Mother of God?" And, while a world waited breathlessly, Mary answered: "Be it done unto me according to thy word" (Lk 1:38). Mary said "yes." That whispered "yes" may well have been, in God's eyes, Mary's finest hour. Why do I say that? Do you remember the woman who cried out to Christ: "Blessed is the womb that bore thee"? Do you remember His answer? "Rather blessed are they who hear the word of God and keep it" (Lk 11:27–28). Hardly a rebuff to His mother; but Jesus does suggest that the real merit of Mary's motherhood lay not simply in giving birth to Him, but in her own lovely response,

"Be it done unto me according to thy word." What someone remarked so strikingly centuries ago: "She conceived Christ in her mind before she conceived Him in her womb."[2]

And so it is with me. In His yearning to make me one with Him, God has already taken the initiative. He took the initiative in my baptism. As He dwelt in Mary's soul from her conception to keep original sin from ever entering it, so He stole into my soul in baptism to take original sin away from it. Of all the countless souls in whom God could have made His home, He chose mine—and left so many souls without Him. He took the initiative in my first Holy Communion. For in Holy Communion I bear heaven within me. Of all the countless souls that could have been fed on the body of Christ, He has chosen to give Himself to me, and has left so many bodies without Him. And one day He will take the initiative once for all. One day from my tomb God will draw a dead body, join to it once more a soul that never died, and God and I will be one forever.

But remember—though God takes the initiative, He always asks one question: "Will you?" In your life there is a daily Angelus—oh, not an angel addressing Mary, but God and His grace tapping at your heart each day—God saying silently every hour you have a choice to make: "Do you *want* God to be formed in your heart this day? Do you *want* to build up in your soul the Christ you received in baptism, the Christ you welcome in Communion? Do you really *want* to fashion Christ in yourself, so that, like our Lady, you can give Him to others, to the countless souls that are shriveled simply because they are Christless? Do you *want* to be one with God, or is there something else you would rather have than Him?" On your response depends your holiness, your union with

2 St. Augustine, Sermon 215, 4 (Patrologia latina 38, 1074).

God. You are one with God only to the extent that you can say sincerely: "Be it done unto me according to thy word."

Briefly, then, what I have insisted on today is this. In devotion to the mother of Christ you are not simply bent low before mystery—mystery that is meaningless as far as your life is concerned. In Mary you glimpse your own destiny—oh, not an immaculate conception, not a virginal motherhood, not even the same glorious assumption. In Mary you glimpse that oneness with God in every phase of your life which is God's dream for you from eternity—a oneness with God which He will work in you through Mary *if*, like that most courageous of women, you will but have the courage to respond: "Be it done unto me according to thy word."

27. The Visitation: Mary's and God's

EVER SINCE the Annunciation thoughtful men and women have wondered what Mary felt, what went on in her mind, when the angel left her—left her with God in her womb. A lovely poem—"After the Annunciation"—has captured this vision of her:

"Mary, the maiden, walked out in the country,
Telling the wheat what the angel had told her;
The bees tumbled out of the flag-flowers to listen,
The birds stopped their fledglings and told them to heed her.

"A woman in blue with wheat to her knees,
Mid a silence of birds and a stillness of bees,
Singing, 'Golden, ah golden, with seedsprays unfurled,
Ripen within me, O wheat of the world!'

"Mary, bluewimpled, walked out in the country,
Telling the vine what none other must know yet;
The butterflies yearned to her hems as to harebells;
The flowers of the bushes fawned softly upon her.

"A woman, gold-wet, with rainbow eyes,
And a border of living butterflies,
Singing, 'Purple, ah purple, with tendrils close curled,
Ripen within me, O vine of the world!' "[1]

[1] Eileen Duggan, "After the Annunciation," in *Poems* (New York: Macmillan, 1939), p. 26.

That is how the poet envisions Mary when first she is alone with the God in her womb. And it may well capture her rapture. It may well be what she *felt*. But the fact is: St. Luke has told us just what our Lady *did* soon after Gabriel left her: "Mary set out in haste . . . into the hill country . . . and greeted Elizabeth" (Lk 1:39–40).

The angel had told Mary two facts: "You shall conceive" and "Your cousin, Elizabeth, has conceived" (Lk 1:31, 36). Her reaction to the first announcement? "Be it done unto me according to thy word" (Lk 1:38). Her reaction to the second? "She set out in haste" (Lk 1:39). Not to test an angel's story; not even with a nose for news. Gabriel had let fall two significant items with respect to Elizabeth: "she who was reproached with barrenness is now in her sixth month" (Lk 1:36). Elizabeth was reproached with barrenness; Mary will congratulate her. Elizabeth is in her sixth month; Mary will help her. The visitation of Mary to Elizabeth is an act of tender human affection, evidence of that selfless self-giving which is God's gift to woman. It portrays our Lady's love not simply for the God within her fashioned to her image, but love too for the human being outside her fashioned to God's image.

But the significant thing is this: the Visitation-scene is not primarily a visitation of Mary; it is a visitation of God. That visitation involves three tremendous ideas: (1) It was *God* who visited His people. (2) The effect of His visitation, and a sign of His coming, was *joy*. (3) That joy flowed from a realization of *redemption*.

The Visitation was a visitation of God. St. Luke tells us: "No sooner had Elizabeth heard Mary's greeting, than the child leaped in her womb; and Elizabeth herself was filled with the Holy Ghost, so that she cried out with a loud voice: 'Blessed art thou among women, and blessed is the fruit of thy womb. How have I deserved to be thus visited by the mother of my Lord?' " (Lk 1:41–43). Mary came, yes; but her role in the Visitation is basically the same as her role in the Incarnation. She bears God for one purpose: to give Him to others. And in this tender scene she brings God to Zachary, to Elizabeth, and to John.

The effect of that visitation, and a sign of God's coming, was joy. Joy not merely in the heart of Mary's cousin. Elizabeth cries: "Why, as soon as ever the voice of thy greeting sounded in my ears, the child in my womb leaped for joy" (Lk 1:44). We have God's word for it that this human being locked six months in the womb of Elizabeth sensed miraculously the presence of his God locked in the womb of Mary. John the Baptist knew that his Lord had come; and he stirred, not as any child stirs within a mother's body—he stirred for joy. His whole being echoed the Magnificat Mary sang at that moment: "My spirit has found joy in God, who is my Saviour" (Lk 1:47).

That joy flowed from a realization of redemption: "God, my Saviour." John's father, Zachary, shouted it three months later when his tongue was loosed and he burst forth with the Benedictus: "Blessed be the Lord, the God of Israel; He has visited His people and wrought their redemption" (Lk 1:68). But, more incredibly still, John himself knew the reason for his joy. We know, beyond dispute, that redemption touched John not in baptism but in his mother's womb. He was sanctified before he was born. When? It seems most likely that original sin left his soul, that God stole into his soul, at the moment of the Visitation: Mary's visitation and God's. That is why he leaped for joy.

And so it is with all humanity; so it is with us. The significance of Mary for us, from the moment of the Annunciation to this very year 1960, is that she brings us Christ. The visitation of Mary is the visitation of God. Through her He came to our world one rapturous midnight; through her He came to Zachary, Elizabeth, and John one joy-rapt day; through her he comes to human souls day after day, time without number. It is all summed up in the Hail Mary. Gabriel begins it: "Hail [Mary], full of grace, the Lord is with thee" (Lk 1:28). Elizabeth continues it: "blessed art thou among women, and blessed is the fruit of thy womb" (Lk 1:42). The Church finishes it: "Holy Mary, Mother of God. . . ."

The effect of God's visitation, and the sign of His coming, is joy. The Church knows this. That is why on the second Sunday of Advent, in the Introit of the Mass, the Church borrows a sentence from the prophet Isaias and trumpets it to the Christian people as they long for Christmas: "People of Sion, look! The Lord shall come to save the nations; and the Lord shall make the glory of His voice heard in the joy of your heart." God's coming brings joy, and joy is a proof that God has come.

If you are a Christian, then your genuine Christmas joy flows from the realization that redemption has touched you— that, if you love God, God loves you, God lives in you. *There* is the joy "no man can take from you" (Jn 16:22). That is the basic reason why a Christian leaps for joy. It is not that you blind yourself to reality, that you close your eyes to poverty and the atom, to Communism and cancer. These will always be as vivid to you as they are to the pagan. And still you can leap for joy. For in the midst of death you have found life, the life brought to you through Mary. For you, as for St. Paul, "life is Christ" (Phil 1:21).

28. The Problem of Loss

THE GOSPELS record several remarkable stories about Mary —about Mary and the God who was her Son. They tell us how Mary gave birth to her God, how she fled with her God, how she gave commands to her God. But the story that interests me at this moment, a story with a strange fascination, is the story how Mary lost her God. I should like you to hear St. Luke tell it.

"Year after year His parents went to Jerusalem for the feast of the Passover. And so, too, when He was twelve years old, they went up according to their custom at the time of the feast. After spending there the required number of days, they prepared to return, but the child Jesus remained behind at Jerusalem, without His parents knowing about it. Supposing Him to be in the caravan, they finished a day's journey, and began to search for Him among their relations and acquaintances. When they did not find Him, they retraced their steps to Jerusalem, there to renew their search for Him. It was only on the third day that they discovered Him in the temple, seated among the rabbis, now listening to them, now asking them questions, while all those that heard Him were charmed by His intelligence and His answers. They were overjoyed to see Him. His mother said to Him: 'Child, why did you behave toward us in this way? Oh, our hearts were heavy—

[159]

your father's and mine—as we searched for you!' He said to
them: 'Why did you search for me? I had to answer my
Father's call, and did you not know it?' But they did not grasp
the meaning of the reply He made to them" (Lk 2:41–50).

The story is fascinating because it contrasts so sharply
with another story, a scene that took place in the same city
twenty years later. As far as our Lord is concerned, the story
is agonizingly long. It is the story of the kiss that betrayed
Him, the slap that stung His cheek, the lash that tore His
back, the thorn that seared His brow; it is the story of the
cross that was His crucifying rest for three hours. As far as
our Lady is concerned, the story is agonizingly brief. St. John
tells it in a single sentence: "There stood beside the cross of
Jesus His mother" (Jn 19:25).

The two scenes—the temple and the cross—are somewhat
the same, yet very different. They are somewhat the same.
Both take place in Jerusalem; in both Mary has lost her Christ;
in both her heart is heavy. But the scenes are strikingly different. In the temple Mary questions her runaway Christ:
"Why? Child, why did you behave toward us in this way?"
On Calvary she utters not a word. In the temple Jesus ex-
plains to her: "I had to answer my Father's call." Beside the
cross no explanation is necessary. In the temple His words
make no sense to her; she does not understand. At the foot
of the cross His silence is eloquent; her understanding is complete.

And *there* is the heart of the matter: understanding. In
the temple our Lady did not understand; we have God's word
for it. She knew she would lose Him as a man; she did not
see why she should lose Him as a child. His behavior at the
age of twelve—she found it as difficult to understand then as
we find it difficult to understand after nineteen centuries. The
redemption of the world through the crucifixion of her Son

she had accepted when she answered "yes" to an angel. What she could not see was a connection between that three-hour agony to come and this three-day absence here and now. And so, from the depths of her anguish, from the fulness of her love, she asked, "Why?"

Beside the cross all is different. No need for words, no need for an anguished "why." Our Lady understands. She will lose Him, but a world will win Him. Through death will come life; through God's death, God's life. And so she is silent, but, like the silence of her Son, so the silence of His mother is eloquent. In the moving language of Pope Pius XII, "as another Eve she offered Him on Golgotha to the Eternal Father for all the children of Adam sin-stained by his fall, and her mother's rights and mother's love were included in the holocaust."[1]

My dear friends in Christ: Part and parcel of human living is the problem of loss. All genuine anguish involves some personal loss. Whatever it is—whether it be death that tears a dear one from me, or illness that eats away my flesh, whether it be ingratitude or infirmity, loneliness or lovelessness that racks my mind and ravages my heart—in all anguish there is something I want and cannot have. It may even seem—and that is the blinding thing about grief, about loss—it may even seem as though the God who is the center of my life is very far from me.

Basically, there are two possible reactions to human anguish, to human loss. The first reaction stems from ignorance, from lack of understanding. I see no rhyme or reason in the sorrow that has touched me: in the accident that has wiped out my family, in the war that has driven a dear one to a strange continent, in the pain that burns my flesh, in this loneliness that is kin to death, in the thousand and one

[1] Pius XII, Encyclical *Mystici corporis* (*Acta apostolicae sedis* 35 [1943] 247).

mysteries that shadow human existence. And, because I do not understand, because I see no reason for all this, from the depths of my anguish I ask, "Why?" Like our Lady in the temple, I ask my God, "Why have you done so to me?"

The second reaction stems not from ignorance but from understanding. Not that I see with perfect clarity how any individual disaster or any global catastrophe fits into God's scheme for human living; I do not. But this I do know. With the crucifixion pain was made precious—my pain. If I stand with Mary, not in the temple but beside the cross, I will understand an incomparable Christian truth, an indispensable Christian fact. In God's wisdom, the way to God is through crucifixion. Pain, my pain, can be redemptive; it can win life, God's life, for me and for those I love. Not because it is pain, but because, like Mary, as I offer Christ on the altar to the Eternal Father for all the children of Adam sin-stained by his fall, I place on the same paten my own body, my own sorrow, my own love. Then, and only then, will that anguished "why" give place to a silence which is eloquent as Mary's, because it means, "I understand." And in that understanding is union, oneness with my crucified God—holiness.

At that moment you may have lost something human; you will have gained something divine. You will have gained . . . God.

29. 🎋 Our Lady's Assumption

MY DEAR friends in Christ: One of the minor mysteries of Mary is: what happened to her after she came slowly down from Calvary? We know that after her Son's death the Apostle John "took her into his own keeping" (Jn 19:27). We know that after her Son's ascension she went with the apostles into Jerusalem's upper room and gave herself up to prayer. We know that, sinless from the very womb of Anne, disease never touched her, that the Mother of God grew old as gracefully as the petals fall from the rose. We know that, like her Son, she "advanced in wisdom with the years, and in favor with God and men" (Lk 2:52). But that is almost all. We are not even certain that she died.

But this much we do know. The God who planned the *first* moment of her earthly existence with such astonishing care, planned the *last* moment with equal care. When He *gave* her to earth, He gave her in a unique way: sinless. When He *took* her from earth, He took her in a unique way: soul and body. In the beginning, her soul did not have to wait through nine long months in a womb before God would come to it; at the end, her body did not have to wait through long years in a tomb before it would come to God. The body that had given Him life, to it the Son of God gave endless life. The flesh from which He Himself took flesh, He took to Himself forever. Briefly, Mary's Immaculate Conception finds its crowning glory in Mary's bodily Assumption.

That idea was expressed more than 1200 years ago by St. John of Damascus in Syria in one of the loveliest paragraphs ever written about our Lady. St. John told the faithful at Gethsemane:

"There was need that this dwelling fit for God be not imprisoned in the hollows of the earth. There was need that she who had entertained God in the guest chamber of her womb, be brought home to the dwelling of her Son. There was need that the body of her who in childbirth had preserved her virginity without stain, be preserved incorrupt even after death. There was need that she who had carried her Creator as a baby on her bosom, should linger lovingly in the dwelling of her God. There was need that she who had looked so closely on her very own Son on the cross, who there felt in her heart the sword-pangs of sorrow which in bearing Him she had been spared, should look upon Him seated with His Father. There was need that the Mother of God should enter into the possessions of her Son and, as Mother of God and handmaid, be reverenced by all creation."[1]

The tender thoughts of John of Damascus were echoed solemnly in 1950 by Pope Pius XII when he said: "By the authority of our Lord Jesus Christ, by the authority of the blessed Apostles Peter and Paul, and by our own authority, we pronounce, declare, and define it to be a dogma divinely revealed that the immaculate Mother of God, the ever-virgin Mary, when the course of her earthly life was run, was assumed to heavenly glory in body and in soul."[2]

That is the naked fact: God took Mary to Himself in

---

[1] St. John Damascene, *Homily 2 on the Falling Asleep of Mary* 14 (*Patrologia graeca* 96, 740-41).

[2] Pius XII, Apostolic Constitution *Munificentissimus Deus* (*Acta apostolicae sedis* 42 [1950] 770).

soul *and* body. But what is the deep significance of the Assumption? This: it gives us a new insight into an old truth. You see, there is a popular misconception among Christians with respect to the human body. For some, the body is nothing but an instrument, a tool of the soul. For others, the body is a necessary evil, a burden from which the soul cries for release. Some Christians have actually held that the body is a punishment, a prison for the soul because the soul sinned in an earlier existence.

Such an attitude pays slender homage to God. It refuses to recognize that the body is an essential part of man, that without the body man is a creature incomplete, man is not fully man, that whether in heaven or purgatory or hell a separated soul, as someone phrased it, "still longs for its body with a purely natural impulse of love."[3]

More than that. In the garden of Eden it was not simply a soul that sinned. It was a human being—Adam—a creature fashioned of soul and body. And as the body played its part in the first sin, as the body fell with the soul from God, so does the body too need redemption. For, when an infant opens his eyes on life, it is not simply his soul that is shriveled— shriveled because it is Godless. His whole being, soul and body, is without God. That is why St. Paul could say: we "groan in our hearts, waiting for that adoption which is the ransoming of our bodies from their slavery" (Rom 8:23).

This redemption of the body, like all redemption, is achieved through the Body of Christ, through the Church. It finds its beginning in baptism. At that instant it is not simply the soul that wakens to the presence of God; it is the whole man. At that instant the body ceases to be what St. Paul termed "the body of death" (Rom 7:24); it comes spiritually

---

[3] Jean Mouroux, *The Meaning of Man*, translated by A. H. G. Downes (New York: Sheed & Ward, 1948), p. 108.

alive, because it too is quickened by the Spirit of God. "Surely you know," Paul reminds us, "that your bodies are the shrines of the Holy Spirit, who dwells in you" (1 Cor 6:19). And, as life goes on, the more fully grace permeates my soul, the more fully my body partakes of redemption, and the less my flesh rebels against the spirit.

But this is only the beginning of redemption. Redemption will find its completion, its perfection, only in the glory of the life to come. Not merely because the soul will see God. From every tomb, from the corners of the earth and the deep of the sea, a body that has rotted will rise, will be transformed into the likeness of Christ's body, and the whole man, soul and body, will confront his Creator in an eternity of knowledge and love.

And that, perhaps more than anything else, is the lesson of our Lady's Assumption. In the eyes of God the human body is a precious thing. So precious that St. Paul could call it a temple of God. So precious that the Church refuses to destroy it even when dead, but blesses it and returns it reverently to the earth from which it was first taken. So precious that God will one day call on His matchless power to restore each human body to the perfection it had here below, and will add to it the glory of His Son's body. In a word: what Mary is, we shall be.

But that truth lays a burden on each Christian. It calls for a state of mind and a way of life; it demands that you be Christian in attitude and in action. The attitude, the state of mind, is . . . reverence. Reverence for a body that can trace its beginnings not merely to mother and father, but to God. Reverence for a body that has housed not merely the soul which gives it human life, but the Lord who graces it with divine life. Reverence for a body that time and again has welcomed the body of Christ. Reverence for a body that is a temple, a little church.

Reverence, yes. But a state of mind is not enough. Reverence in attitude calls for reverence in action. In this connection I would simply remind you that there are *seven* deadly sins —sins that are deadly not only because they rain death on the soul, but because they can degrade the whole man, body too. Not sex lust alone, but the animal lust for food and drink, for lavish living, for glory and applause; the anger that flushes the flesh and the envy that is like a cancer within; the lukewarmness for God that will not battle against the body's drag, the lukewarmness that moved God to say: "Being what thou art, lukewarm, neither cold nor hot, thou wilt make me vomit thee out of my mouth" (Ap 3:16).

Dear friends in Christ: It is the whole man, soul and body, that must live *for* God today; because it is the whole man, soul and body, that will live *with* God forever. What Mary is, we shall be.

The Theological Virtues

30. ✿ I Believe!

More than fifteen hundred years ago St. Augustine revealed a remarkable insight into our Lady. "Mary," he insisted, "was more blessed because she laid hold of faith in Christ than because she conceived the flesh of Christ. . . . Her motherly relationship to Him would have been of no use to Mary, had she not carried Christ in her heart more happily even than she carried Him in her womb." She "conceived Christ in her mind before she conceived Him in her womb." "It was by faith she gave Him birth, it was by faith she conceived Him."[1]

The crucial hour of our Lady's life was the Annunciation. That scene was a critical scene in the drama of redemption. On the stage three characters stood: a divine person, an angelic messenger, a human being. God, Gabriel, Mary. And the central issue was . . . faith.

Gabriel asked Mary to believe that he was a messenger from the face of God, not a devil from the depths of hell. He asked her to take it on God's word that she would conceive a child, yet not of a human father; that this child would come into existence in that the Holy Spirit, the Third Person of the Trinity, would somehow come upon her; that this child would be not a mere man but the God-man, God in human flesh.

[1] St. Augustine, De sancta virginitate 3 (Patrologia latina 40, 398); Sermon 215, 4 (Patrologia latina 38, 1074).

Yes, God asked Mary to believe that for nine months she would carry beneath her heart a divine infant, as other Jewish women carried a sheerly human infant. He may even have asked her to believe more: That in her home, under her care, God would grow, God would eat and sleep and work and study. That she would teach the God of Love how to love God. That one day God would leave her, because He had a mission from above, a world to win. That He would come to His own, and His own would give Him no welcome. That God would be sold for silver and nailed to wood. That she would stand beneath His cross, with a sword in her heart. That He would be laid in a tomb, and she would return home, there to wait till He rose from the dead.

That, briefly, is what Mary was asked to believe. An incredible burden for a teen-age girl, a child of fourteen or fifteen. In her, at that moment, were centered "the hopes and fears of all the years." Her answer? While a world waited in breathless anguish, Mary replied, "Be it done unto me according to thy word" (Lk 1:38). Mary said, "I believe." Mary murmured, "yes."

That murmured yes was a remarkable thing, on four counts. It was remarkable, in the first place, because the answer did not come easily. When the angel addressed her, "Hail, full of grace," St. Luke tells us "she was much perplexed at hearing him speak so, and cast about in her mind, what she was to make of such a greeting" (Lk 1:28–29). She was not naive, blissfully ignorant, unaware of life. When Gabriel announced, "You will conceive," she put a direct question to him: "How can that be, since I have no knowledge of man?" (Lk 1:31, 34).

That murmured yes was a remarkable thing, secondly, because she could have said no. Like the rich young man in the Gospel to whom Christ confided, "If you want to be perfect, go home, sell what you have, give it to the poor, then come back and follow me," like him Mary too could have "walked away sad at heart" (Mt 19:21–22) : this is too much to ask of flesh and blood. Like the disciples to whom Christ promised His flesh for food, His blood as drink, Mary too could have answered, "This is a hard saying. Who can listen to it?" And like them she too could have gone "back to [her] old ways, and walked no more in [God's] company" (Jn 6:61, 67).

That murmured yes was a remarkable thing, thirdly, because it was a total yes. She believed everything God had revealed to her. She believed the incredible as well as the believable, the sad tidings as well as the glad. She did not pick and choose: I will take Bethlehem's crib, but not Calvary's cross. I will take the thirty years in Nazareth, but not the exile to Egypt. I will be His mother at Cana, but not in Gethsemane. No. She believed she would be mother not simply of God, but of God crucified. She believed not only that her God would live within her, but that He would die apart from her.

That murmured yes was a remarkable thing, finally, because it rested on God's word alone. She believed everything Gabriel told her, not because *she saw* it would be so, but because *God said* it was to be so. That is why her act of faith was a resounding thing: "Be it done unto me!" That is why there was joy in her faith, joy unconfined: "My spirit has found joy in God, my Saviour" (Lk 1:47). At that moment she who had conceived Christ in her mind conceived Christ in her body. At that moment she was supremely holy: she was one with her God.

My dear friends: A scene very like the Annunciation takes place in your heart. Your life is the drama of redemption all over again. On the stage three characters stand: a divine

[173]

person, a messenger from God, a human being. Christ, the Church, you. Like an angel from the face of God, the Church stands before you, the agent of Christ's revelation. She tells you what you must believe if you are to conceive Christ and bring Him to birth in your soul. Much that she proposes is as difficult as the tidings brought to Mary. There is but one God, who is three Persons. . . . God's Son was born of a virgin, died between thieves. . . . The white wafer that looks like bread, that feels like bread, that tastes like bread, is not bread; it is God enfleshed. . . . At the dawn of life a little water flows and a baby becomes God's child. . . . In the midst of life God's life courses through my soul like another bloodstream. . . . In the evening of life, life is not taken away, life is but changed. . . . A human being who dies with face turned from God will burn endlessly in hell. . . . The man and woman whom God has bound together, let no man break asunder. . . . He who looks on a woman to lust after her has already committed adultery with her in his heart. . . .

These, and a hundred other truths, you are asked to believe. An incredible burden for a human being, a creature fashioned of flesh and blood. Your answer? In virtue of a God-given gift, the gift of faith, you trumpet each day your act of faith: "I believe!"

That resounding yes is a remarkable thing, on four counts. It is remarkable, in the first place, because, as with Mary, the answer does not come easily. The learned world laughs at you; the Communist world thirsts for your blood; your friends pity you; your mind asks questions; your very flesh rises in rebellion. And still you say, "I believe."

That resounding yes is a remarkable thing, secondly, because, like Mary, you can say no. There is no persecutor's fire to burn faith into you, no rack to force faith from your lips. You can thunder, "I do *not* believe," and you have nothing to lose—nothing except God.

That resounding yes is a remarkable thing, thirdly, because, like Mary's, it is a total yes: "I believe everything, all the truths which the Church teaches." You believe the incredible as well as the believable, the sad tidings as well as the glad. You do not pick and choose: "I believe divorce is wrong, but not in my case. . . . I believe in actual sin, but not in original sin. . . . I just won't believe that God would punish anybody forever. . . . The Church is a little 'off' on sex. . . ." No. The message is God's message. The whole message. Believe it all, or believe none of it. Deny any iota, and logically you must deny it all.

That resounding yes is a remarkable thing, finally, because, like Mary's, your act of faith is uttered on God's word alone. "I believe all the truths which the Church teaches, because thou hast revealed them." The Church is but a messenger; the message is God's. The Church's function is Gabriel's: she bears witness to her Lord. She says simply: "This is the mind of God; this is His will." As Mary said yes not so much to Gabriel as to God, so your act of faith is murmured not to the Church but to Christ.

My dear friends: Holiness is oneness with God. It depends on two factors: God's initiative, your response. The extent of your holiness depends in great measure on your response to the gift of faith—on the completeness with which you can answer, "I believe." Only then will you, like Mary, realize what it means to conceive Christ within you; only then will you cry with Mary, "My spirit has found *joy* in God, my Saviour."

31. They No Longer Have Hope

IN RECENT days a French journalist wrote: "Concentration camps still exist. The numbers of refugees from China, Korea, Palestine, Hungary, Czechoslovakia and Germany continue to increase; thousands of human beings who have done nothing more than live normally, in average fashion, like any of us. They were neither very good nor very bad. They were average men. And now they have lost everything; they are wounded but they no longer have the strength to cry out; they merely exist. Death, identification tags, rape, separations are finally accepted as the normal thing by them. They no longer have hope."[1]

They no longer have hope. Perhaps the saddest words in the world—because they are the epitaph of despair. A man without hope is a man without life. It has always been so. It was so with our first father, when God exiled Adam from Eden, told him that divine life had left him and human life would leave him. It was so with the two disciples who left Jerusalem after the crucifixion of their Life: "we had hoped" (Lk 24:21). It is so even now, wherever men have stolen from men their reason for living.

What, then, is this precious thing that spells the difference

[1] Bertrand Schneider, "East German Refugees," *The Commonweal 55*, no. 18 (Feb. 8, 1952), 439.

between life and death? What is hope? Oh, not the imitation that passes for hope today, but the real thing, hope in a Christ-redeemed world. The answer is discoverable in St. Paul's Letter to the Romans—four incisive sentences: "Our salvation is founded upon the hope of something. But hope would not be hope at all if its object were in view. And if we are hoping for something still unseen, then we need endurance to wait for it. Only, the Spirit comes to the aid of our weakness" (Rom 8:24–26).

These four statements reveal four facets of Christian hope, and these are the four points I shall sketch today. St. Paul tells us (1) that the object of Christian hope is God—God face to face; (2) that God is not yet our face-to-face possession; (3) that, precisely because God is still unseen, our way to God lies through shadows and distress; and (4) that the reason for our hope is that, at every step to the vision of God, God is present invisibly. In brief, Paul tells us: hope is, because God is.

First, then, "our salvation is founded upon the hope of something." Christian hope is a very definite thing. It is the Christian's confident yearning, his confident expectation, his confident straining for the Good, for the God, for whom he was made. The catechism tells you: in hope you "firmly trust that God will give" you "eternal life and the means to obtain it." You who die linked to your Lord in love will be unbelievably alive. Alive in mind; for, as Paul phrased it, "At present, we are looking at a confused reflection in a mirror; then, we shall see face to face; now, I have only glimpses of knowledge; then, I shall recognize God as He has recognized me" (1 Cor 13:12). Alive in love; for, as St. John put it, "We are children of God even now; what we shall be hereafter, has not yet been made known. But we know that when He comes we shall be like Him" (1 Jn 3:2). Alive at last in body too—the same body as now, but without the pain, without the tears. Faith tells you that this is your destiny; hope assures you that this will be yours!

The second point: "hope would not be hope at all if its object were in view," if God were already within our grasp. Dante, you may remember, has a famous line: "All hope abandon, ye who enter here."[2] That legend Dante wrote over the gates of hell. Why? Because the hellishness of hell is the annihilation of hope. Strangely enough, the same words could just as easily be written over the gates of heaven: "All hope abandon, ye who enter here." Just as there is no hope in hell, so there is no hope in heaven—but for a different reason. In hell there is no possibility of hope, because what you once hoped for you can never possess. In heaven there is no need of hope, because what you once hoped for you now possess— forever.

That brings up Paul's third point: "if we are hoping for something unseen, then we need endurance to wait for it." Precisely because God is as yet unseen, our way to God lies through shadows and distress. For each of us there is a concrete path over which our hope travels. It is built up of little things: this fleeting moment, this foxhole, this smile or this tear, this desire, this decision—anything and everything of which I can whisper: "Thy will be done." But here is the agony of hope: as long as there is hope, there will also be fear —fear of that awesome ability I have to say "no," to shout out: "Not thy will but mine be done!" "Without me," the Son of God insisted, "you can do nothing" (Jn 15:5). Of yourself you can only say: "I will *not* serve."

But here, St. Paul concludes, "the Spirit comes to the aid of our weakness." The reason for Christian hope is this: at every stage to the vision of God, God is present invisibly. The

---

2 Dante, *Divina commedia: Inferno*, Canto 3.

real tragedy of hope today is not that so many millions have no hope at all. The soul that has been stripped naked and leveled to the earth may well be the seed-plot of hope; its salvation may flow from its tears, from what Tennyson called "tears from the depth of some divine despair."[3] The modern tragedy is that so many millions live in hope—a hope that is not grounded in God. They are incurable optimists; there is always a solution just around the corner: a drug, a stockpile, an armistice, an election. But the optimism is unchristian:

> "The worldly hope men set their hearts upon
> Turns ashes—or it prospers; and anon,
> Like snow upon the desert's dusty face
> Lighting a little hour or two—is gone."[4]

The Christian hopes for God *from God*: "In thee, O Lord, have I hoped . . ." (Ps 30:2). Anything that is a step toward the vision of God—be it shrouded in suffering or haloed with joy—anything that brings me a little closer to my destiny is a gift of God—a gift that God is free to refuse. The point is, God will not refuse His help. How do we know that?

There is a remarkable passage in the New Testament, in the Letter to the Hebrews. "Our great longing is to see you all showing the same eagerness—the same eagerness you show in works of charity—show the same eagerness right up to the end, looking forward to the fulfilment of your hope." Why? Because to Abraham and to us God made a promise: the promise of Christ and of life without end through Christ. More than that. "Men will confirm their word by oath, which puts an end to all controversy. God, in the same way, eager to convince [us] that His design was irrevocable, pledged Himself by an oath. Two irrevocable assurances"—God's promise

---

3 Alfred Lord Tennyson, *The Princess*, Part 4, Song, Stanza 1.

4 *The Rubaiyat of Omar Khayyam* 14, translated by Edward Fitzgerald (New York: Three Sirens Press, 193?), p. 48.

and God's oath—"over which there could be no question of God deceiving us, were to bring firm confidence to us poor castaways, bidding us cling to the hope we have in view, the anchorage of our souls" (Heb 6:11-19).

For a Christian the song of hope is the song of the Psalmist: "Let me sing of thy mercy, high above heaven itself; of thy faithfulness, that reaches the clouds" (Ps 107:4-5). For the very power to hope was God's birthday gift to you: at your baptism God poured into your soul the power to walk in the midst of the shadow of death and to fear no evil—because He is with you.

I began with a prison of despair; let me end in a prison of hope. In April, 1951, a message reached Rome from a subterranean cell in Rumania. It was a message from a priest, and it ran in part like this:

"I reached my prison on the afternoon of the day of my arrest. How long ago that was . . . I don't know, because I am always in the dark. On that day, in complete darkness, I was led to this cell. When the door closed behind me, through God's mercy I was thinking of God, and remembered to offer up my troubles for His glory, so that my humiliation was filled with God's glory and became an immediate comfort to my soul. . . .

"I thought with horror that sometimes it is easier to resist actual pain and bodily wounds than the wave of sickness that assails one's stomach at a foul smell. I dreaded the possibility that I might weaken, and through God's mercy I was able to concentrate upon God, and it pleased God to fill my cell with an infinitesimal but overbrimming small part of His great glory. . . .

"Believe me . . . all of you who are outside, there is a face of the cross which cannot be apprehended save by those who lie in jail. There is a part of the living God which is only

[181]

known to those who are themselves hidden in some subterranean cell, in darkness and in chains. There may be happiness in the light which streams through a small barred window of an above-ground prison cell, but God's happiness rests longer upon those who have not light's distraction.

"God, in His mercy, beat at my door, and the All Highest entered without keys. I recite the rosary—the glorious mysteries—and I know our Lady is a comforter to the afflicted, and often my lips cannot form the words because my heart is overfull. . . ."[5]

Dear friends in Christ: Must we be stripped naked and leveled to the earth before we begin to hope like Christians? Before we hope *for God* . . . *from God?*

[5] *Time*, Apr. 30, 1951, pp. 71–72.

32. Three Levels of Love

In his remarkable little book of *Spiritual Exercises*, St. Ignatius Loyola sketches what he calls "three degrees of humility."[1] In point of fact, these three degrees of humility are three degrees of submission to God's will, three degrees in man's return of love for love. The first degree of submission to God's will is the *essence* of love; the second is the *logic* of love; and the third is the *folly* of love. It is these three levels of love that I would offer you today.

"The first degree of humility," Ignatius tells us, "is necessary for eternal salvation. It is, that I so submit and humble myself, as far as I can, in all things to obey the law of God our Lord, that even though men should make me lord of all created things in this world, or for the sake of my own temporal life, I would not enter into deliberation about breaking a commandment, whether divine or human, which bound me under mortal sin." That, as Ignatius saw it, is the essence, the minimum, of love; without that, there is no genuine love. I love God at least this much: there is nothing, there is no one, in this world so attractive that for it or for him or for her I would offend God seriously.

To grasp that, you must grasp what sin is and what love

---

[1] *The Text of the Spiritual Exercises of Saint Ignatius* (4th ed. rev.; Westminster, Md.: Newman, 1943), pp. 52-53.

is. To see what sin is, see what sin does. In the pages of Scripture there are four remarkable passages which tell us vividly what sin does. The first passage is a sentence of Christ in the Gospel of Luke: "I saw Satan fall like lightning from heaven" (Lk 10:18). For one serious sin God created hell; for a single act of disobedience God cast from Him a host of angels forever.

The second passage is a judgment of God in Genesis: "Because you have eaten of the tree whereof I commanded you that you should not eat, cursed is the earth in your work. . . . In the sweat of your face shall you eat bread till you return to the earth out of which you were taken; for dust you are, and into dust you shall return" (Gn 3:17, 19). For one serious sin the first human being lost God's life and his own life; with a single act of disobedience Adam left us a terrifying legacy: sin, concupiscence, death.

The third passage is a sentence from St. Mark: "Jesus cried out with a loud voice and expired" (Mk 15:37). If you want to see what sin does, kneel down on Calvary: sin nailed the Son of God to wood.

The fourth passage is a judgment of God in St. Matthew: "Then [the King] will say to those on His left hand: 'Depart from me, cursed ones, into everlasting fire, which was prepared for the devil and his angels'" (Mt 25:41). For one serious sin unrepented, unforgiven, a human being will be separated from his God forever.

It is obvious, I think, that sin offends God. The first degree of submission to God's will is this: I will never deliberately consider offending God in a serious matter. The lowest level of genuine love is this: the lover refuses to offend the beloved. A child cannot strike his mother and protest that he loves her. A husband cannot coldbloodedly commit adultery and claim at that moment that he loves his wife. A human being cannot say to his God, "I will not serve," and cry with his next breath, "I love you." To love God is to be one with God; in sin you are divorced from God.

The answer to sin is love. To love God is to do God's will; love dares not offend. Remember Christ's solemn declaration the night before His crucifixion: "He who has my commandments and keeps them, he it is who loves me" (Jn 14:21). There, on God's own word, there is the link between love and submission, between love and sinlessness; there is the first degree of Ignatian humility; there is the essence of love: I will not offend my beloved, the God I love. This is the basic response of the Christian to his Lord, the response crystallized in the Prayer for Generosity that supposedly fell from the lips of Ignatius:

"Dearest Lord, teach me to be generous. Teach me to serve thee as thou deservest: to give and not to count the cost; to fight and not to heed the wounds; to toil and not to seek for rest; to labor and not ask for reward, save that of knowing that I am doing thy will."

That is the lowest level of genuine love: I will not offend. But Ignatius mounts one step higher: "The second degree is more perfect than the first. It consists in this, that I will never enter into deliberation about committing a venial sin, neither for the sake of all created things, nor even if on that account men should deprive me of life." The second level of love is a higher level. Love is not content simply because it does not offend; love is impatient to please. And that is the logic of love.

The most startling example, in all human history, of love's anxiety to please is God in flesh. The moving force of His life was a sentence that fell from His lips: "The things that please my Father I do always" (Jn 8:29). Because it pleased His Father, He was born of a Jewish girl, fled like a refugee, worked and prayed and hungered, breathed His last breath imprisoned with nails. In the life of our Lord there is no anguished questioning: "What *must* I do if I am not to *lose* my Father's love?" That is the lowest level of love, its bare essence. If love is to be not merely genuine but logical, the lover says of the beloved: "The things that please him I do always."

That love of our Lord for His Father, that passion to please, is reflected in our own experience. I am thinking of a friend, a successful businessman, a remarkably devout Catholic, who has been married forty years. After forty years he still greets his wife with an affectionate kiss after each separation, no matter how short. He still seats her at table in their own home, though there be no one to see. He still offers her his arm as they walk, though she needs it not. There is a corsage for every day that has special meaning; there is a gift, small but precious, for every anniversary. Above all, there is a gentleness of speech, a reverence in attitude, which is a living proof of the love that is deep within. "The things that please her I do always." It is the logic of love; for, if you are genuinely in love, you will never be satisfied simply because you have not lost the object of your love; your concern will be to please.

And that is the love I would have blossom in your heart towards God. It is simply the realization of our Lord's command: "Thou shalt love the Lord thy God with thy *whole* heart, and with thy *whole* soul, and with thy *whole* mind, and with thy *whole* strength" (Mk 12:30). That sort of love is utterly logical. After all, you have your Beloved, you have God, within you. You welcomed Him initially in your baptism; you welcome Him in each Communion; you welcome Him with each whisper that reveals your faith, your hope, your love, your sorrow. In a word, the God you love is a living, quickening reality within you.

But, at the moment, I am not afraid you will *lose* Him; I am afraid you may not *please* Him. I am afraid your attitude may not be the attitude of Ignatius' second degree of submission: "I will never enter into deliberation about committing a venial sin, neither for the sake of all created things, nor even if on that account men should deprive me of life." I am afraid that, if the pressure is heavy enough, you *will* tell the little white lie. I am afraid that, if you are fearful of what people may say about you, you *will* listen to the off-color joke, the groundless gossip, the uncharitable chit-chat. I am afraid that, if you are not careful, you *may* harbor in your heart just a little bit of anger, of envy, of sloth, of covetousness, of pride, of gluttony, of lust. In brief, I am afraid that you may not give *all* your love to God, simply because it is much easier not to. And if you do not give God your *whole* heart, then your love may be genuine but it is not logical; for this is the God who loves you with an everlasting love, an infinite love, a crucified love. This is the Love who lives within you. This is your happiness, now and forever.

The second degree of submission to God's will, the second level of love in return for love, is summed up in a prayer of Ignatius, a companion piece to the Prayer for Generosity:

"Take, O Lord, and receive all my liberty, my memory, my understanding, and all my will, whatsoever I have and possess. Thou hast given all these things to me; to thee, O Lord, I restore them. All are thine; dispose of them all according to thy will. Give me thy love and thy grace, for this is enough for me."[2]

The first level of love is this: I will not offend God. The second level of love is this: I want to please God. The third, the highest, level of love is this: I want to be like God. Listen to Ignatius: "The third degree is the most perfect: the better

2 *Ibid.*, p. 75.

to imitate Christ our Lord, and to become actually more like to Him, I desire and choose rather poverty with Christ poor than riches; contempt with Christ contemned than honors; and I desire to be esteemed as useless and foolish for Christ's sake, who was first held to be such, than to be accounted wise and prudent in this world."

If the first level is the essence of love, if the second level is the logic of love, then the third level is the folly of love, love's madness. Why? Because it means I want to be like the one I love—but in this case the Beloved is crucified.

There are two basic facts here. The first basic fact is God's love for you. It is the pithy insight of St. Paul: "He loved me and gave Himself up for me" (Gal 2:20). He loved me. . . . At this point I am not concerned with the naked truth of God's love: the realization that just as God is Intelligence with a capital I, so too He must be Love with a capital L. Nor am I concerned with any and every expression of God's love, be it as captivating as creation: "I have loved thee with an everlasting love, therefore have I drawn thee" (Jer 31:3). What must sear your souls here is a truth which to the unbeliever must always smack of blasphemy, of contradiction: God's love literally crucified Him.

"No form was His, no beauty, that we should gaze at Him;
    No comeliness, that we should desire Him.
Despised was He, and the réfuse of men,
    A man of sorrows. . . ."

(Is 53:2–3)

More astonishingly still, the love that crucified Him reaches out to *me*—as surely as it reached out to the mother who cradled Him and the disciple who rested his head on His heart: "He loved me and gave Himself up for me." It reaches out to each of us.

"He was pierced for our transgressions,

He was bruised for our misdoings;
The penalty of our peace lay upon Him,
And by His stripes there was healing for us."

(Is 53:5)

The second basic fact is this: what will be your return of love? In the first place, I would ask you not to resent crucifixion when it comes. It is not only the first Christ who is meaningless without His cross. Every Christ since Calvary must, to some extent, share the crucifixion of which Christianity was born. Poverty, contempt, uselessness—whatever it be, carry the cross not like Simon of Cyrene, reluctantly, but like Jesus of Nazareth, gladsomely.

Secondly, if with God's grace you are strong enough, I would have you *ask* for this highest level of love; I would have you *ask*, with Ignatius, to be poor with Christ poor, to be despised with Christ despised, to be accounted useless and foolish for His sake. Do not ask for it lightly. It is love supreme, yes; for it means that you want to be like, utterly like, the God you love. But this likeness for which you yearn is a frightening sort of likeness: in this instance the One you love is pinned to a cross. It involves a third prayer, a prayer suggested by St. Ignatius, the prayer to be received under the standard of the Crucified:

"Dear God, I ask to be received under your standard. And first, in the highest degree of poverty of spirit, and not less in actual poverty, if it please your divine majesty and you should choose to elect and receive me to it. Secondly, in bearing reproaches and insults, the better to imitate you in these, provided only I can endure them without sin on the part of any person, or displeasure to your divine majesty."[3]

That, my dear friends in Christ, that is sanctity—at its highest.

3 *Ibid*, p. 47.

33. Love One Another

ALL THE world knows the story of Father Damien of Molokai. Here was a man who left his native Belgium at twenty-three for the Hawaiian missions. Why? Because he saw the image of God in his fellow men. Here was a man who volunteered for a leper island. Why? His bishop told the lepers why, when he took Damien to Molokai:

"So far, my children, you have been left alone and uncared for. But you shall be so no longer. I have brought you one who will be a father to you, and who loves you so much that for your welfare and for the sake of your immortal souls, he does not hesitate to become one of you; to live and die with you."[1]

Here was a man who brought love to a colony where the law was, "In this place there is no law." The air he breathed was rotting flesh; he washed sores and bandaged wounds; he cut off dead limbs; he buried lepers with his own hands. And one day, aged forty-five, he walked from the altar to the sanctuary rail after the Gospel, paused a moment, looked at his audience, and then—instead of the usual "My brethren," he said slowly and lovingly, "We lepers." Damien had contracted the disease of the people he loved. "We lepers."[2]

In the magnificent discourse which the Son of God pre-

[1] John Farrow, *Damien the Leper* (New York: Sheed & Ward, 1937), p. 84.
[2] Cf. *ibid.*, p. 156.

sented to His disciples at the Last Supper, one of the more significant features was what He called a "new commandment": "A new commandment I give you, that you love one another: that as I have loved you, you also love one another. By this will all men know that you are my disciples, if you have love for one another" (Jn 13:34–35). In the striking language of Christ, that new commandment has three facets —and those three facets are the three points I shall make this evening: (1) "as I have loved you"; (2) "so you also love one another"; (3) "by this will all men know that you are my disciples."

First, then: "as I have loved you." If there is one idea which sums up the Incarnation and the redemption, if there is one fact that gives meaning to God's advent on earth, it is God's love for man. St. John put it magnificently when he wrote: "God so loved the world that He gave His only Son" (Jn 3:16). St. Paul phrased it even more simply when he said: "He loved me" (Gal 2:20).

That love laid the Son of God within a Virgin's womb and nine months later in a feeding trough. That love made God obedient for thirty years to two of His own creatures. That love kindled three years of ceaseless "compassion on the crowd" (Mt 15:32), compassion for all manner of suffering: for leprosy and hunger and debt, for blindness and bewilderment, for the fever that burns the flesh and the bereavement that blunts the spirit. That love made Him choose a cross for the world's redemption. Not that the world could not have been redeemed from a crib in Bethlehem or a boat on the Sea of Galilee; but because He was fired by His own tremendous assertion: "Greater love than this no man hath, that a man lay down his life for his friends" (Jn 15:13). That love is alive today. It is alive within every drop of water that gives God's life to a newborn child; it lives on the lips of every priest who whispers, "I absolve you"; it hovers over each Christian who receives the body and blood of his God; it transforms marriage into a sacrament where husband gives to wife, wife gives to husband, the wedding gift of grace, God to dwell in each other's soul; it will transfigure the oil that last anoints you, so that in the life to come you may share God's love days without end. Little wonder that St. John begins the account of the passion with the inspired sentence: "Before the feast of the Passover, Jesus, knowing that His hour had come, to pass out of this world to the Father, having loved His own who were in the world, loved them to the end" (Jn 13:1), loved them to perfection.

So much for my first point: "as I have loved you." My second point: "so you also love one another." To love is to give—to give myself and what is mine. To love perfectly is to give till there is nothing left to give—to give unto death: "Greater love than this no man hath." That is the way Christ our Lord loved—a God who, knowing the tragedy as well as the sublimity of His love, gave His life gladly for the human beings He had shaped in His image. That is how Damien loved—a man who, knowing full well the price of his love, became literally a leper among the lepers he loved. That is how, on God's own word, every Christian is expected to love: "as I have loved you." You are more like Christ, and therefore more genuinely Christian, the more your love resembles His love who gave His life not merely for His Mother Mary and St. John, but for the Judas who sold Him and the Peter who disowned Him, for the Herod who made sport of Him and the Pilate who washed His hands of Him, for the servant who slapped His face and the soldier who nailed His hands to the wood.

Do not tell me it is impossible. We have seen it in Damien the leper. We saw it in the Second World War, in the four chaplains who drowned arm-in-arm because they had given their lifebelts to others. We see it in a mother's burning yearning: to take to herself the cancer that eats her child, to give her life that a dear one may live.

But, at the moment, my concern is not, are you willing to *die* for love? My concern is, are you willing to *live* in love? The problem is not that there are so few Christians who love perfectly; the problem is rather that there are so many Christians who hate intensely. There are Christians who are bitter as bile if they see joy in another's eyes, good health in another's body, honor in another's career, prosperity in another's home. There are Christians who are happiest when they can scatter doubt on another's virtue, another's honesty, another's motives. There are Christians whose love is limited to their own country, their own creed, their own color. There are even a few Christians who will murder a fellow Christian rather than ride side-by-side with him.

I am asking you tonight to begin to love one another as Christ has loved you. I am asking you to tear hate and envy out of your hearts, to give something of yourself to every human being who enters your little world, to pray God's blessing on the Judas who has betrayed you and the Herod who has laughed at you and the Pilate who has washed his hands of you. God does not ask you to *like* them, but He does insist that you *love* them. Love them not with the surface love that means moonlight and roses, but with the true love that wills what God knows is best for them, that prays what is for their genuine happiness, that does something concrete to realize it. Remember that hate is a spawn of hell; for hate was born of the devil, and hate will live on in eternity only in hell. Be afraid not to love those whom Christ Himself loves because they are sons of the same Father. In short, love one another as He has loved you.

My last point, briefly: "By this will all men know that you are my disciples, if you have love for one another." History tells us that in the Church's infancy one of the most compelling arguments for Christianity was the love which Christians lavished on one another. So striking was it, so genuine, that it forced from the lips of pagans the deathless exclamation, "See how these Christians love one another!" Is that tribute still true? Is my love so strong, so all-embracing, that in me my neighbor can spy Christ?

If it is not, if my love is but a flickering flame, if my heart is a storehouse of old injuries and a nursery of revenge, it might be wise to meditate the strong language of St. John, the apostle of love: "If anyone says, 'I love God,' and hates his brother, he is a liar" (1 Jn 4:20).

Eschatology or The Last Things

34. Greater Love Than This No Man Hath

THAT REMARKABLE play, *Cyrano de Bergerac*, has a touching fifth act. The scene is laid in a garden, a convent garden. It is late October. Above the still living green of the turf all the foliage is red and yellow and brown—but everywhere the leaves are falling. Cyrano, in his life's last hour, murmurs to Roxane: "The leaves. . . ." Roxane raises her head, looks away through the trees: "What color—perfect Venetian red! Look at them fall." "Yes," says Cyrano:

> "Yes—they know how to die. A little way
> From the branch to the earth, a little fear
> Of mingling with the common dust—and yet
> They go down gracefully—a fall that seems
> Like flying!"[1]

"They know how to die." For three years, over this station, I have tried to tell you how to live. This afternoon I should like to tell you how to die. It is quite important, if only because to know how to die is to know how to live. I shall stress three ideas: (1) In the eyes of a human being, death is a fact. (2) In the eyes of a Christian, death is a punishment. (3) In the eyes of a saint, death is an act of love.

[1] Edmond Rostand, *Cyrano de Bergerac*, translated by Brian Hooker (New York: Modern Library [Random House], n. d.), pp. 304-5.

First, then: In the eyes of a human being, death is a fact. At rock bottom, death does not depend on your philosophy; it is not the plaything of your ideas. One day, that fragile, enigmatic thing called life will leave you. One day, that extraordinary element within you which can fashion a tear-drop or sculpture a smile, which can frame the formula for an atom bomb or range through history and over oceans with the speed of light—that element will escape from you, and leave only the speechless, lifeless, depressing thing we call a dead body. There is no eluding it. You may sleep or dance it out of mind; you cannot sleep or dance it out of existence. Death plays no favorites. Unlike the avenging angel of Exodus, it does not pass God's chosen people by, to fasten on infidels; it sweeps away beauty as well the beast. In death's dread uncertainties—when? how? where?—one thing is dreadfully certain: you *will* die.

Death is a fact—perhaps the most difficult fact you must face. Death is hard, and you do not want to die. Not so much because you are afraid of that plunge into darkness. Death is hard, because death means separation; it is an end. You do not want to die, because you must leave what you love behind you. And that is torment even for a creature who loves his Lord dearly. For, as the poet, Francis Thompson, put it:

> ". . . though I knew His love Who followed,
> Yet was I sore adread
> Lest, having Him, I must have naught beside."[2]

If you would glimpse how difficult death can be, kneel by the God-man in the garden of Gethsemane, watch His sweat become as drops of blood, and listen to His prayer: "Father, if it be possible, let this chalice pass from me" (Mt 26:39).

---

2 Francis Thompson, "The Hound of Heaven," ed. Wilfred Meynell, *op. cit.,* p. 107.

The chalice did not pass from Him; and the chalice will not pass from you.

In the eyes of a human being, death is a fact. In the eyes of a Christian, death is a punishment—a punishment for sin. You see, in God's plan for man there was no place for death. When God shaped the first human being, He had in mind for you and me a destiny literally deathless. There would be birth, yes; growth, yes; life and love, yes; but death, never! A short span of burning yearning for God, and God would take us to Himself, without pain, without tears. It all rested with the first human being, with Adam. One command God gave him: "Thou mayest eat thy fill of all the trees in the garden except the tree which brings knowledge of good and evil; if ever thou eatest of this, thy doom is death" (Gn 2:16–17). Adam ate; and God trumpeted to him, and through him to us: "Thou shalt earn thy bread with the sweat of thy brow, until thou goest back into the ground from which thou wast taken; dust thou art, and unto dust thou shalt return" (Gn 3:19). Briefly, God told Adam, and He told us: life would leave his body, because love had fled from his soul.

In the eyes of a human being, death is a fact of life. In the eyes of a Christian, death is a punishment for sin. But in the eyes of a saint, death is an act of love.

Several weeks ago the American people were startled by a newspaper story. A young priest, a gallant ex-chaplain, lay dying of cancer in a hospital in Kansas. When a reporter came round to see him, he spoke of his death as calmly as if he were being assigned a new post. But the sentence that mystified America was fashioned of nine simple words, whose sincerity could not be denied: "I consider it a privilege to die of cancer."

My dear friends: For the human being who knows God and loves Him, the mystery is no mystery at all. You see, to live Christianity is to live Christ. "For me," as St. Paul put it, "life *is* Christ" (Phil 1:21). But there is little point to reproducing in your lives the life of Christ, unless you somehow reproduce in your death the death of Christ. And the death of Christ, like His life, can be summed up in one word: sacrifice.

That sacrifice was compounded of two elements: an offering and an immolation. It involved, in the first place, an offering—the gift our Lord made of Himself the eve of His crucifixion: "This is my body, which is offered for you. This is my blood, which is poured out for you" (Lk 22:19–20; Mt 26:26–28). Each Christian who loves his Lord dearly must make a like offering, a like gift of himself to God: "This is my body, which is offered to you. This is my blood, which is poured out for you." That offering, with all it implies, is renewed each dawn by the Catholic who whispers: "I offer thee my prayers, works, joys, and sufferings of this day."

Our Lord's offering involved an immolation. I mean a day-by-day passion from crib to cross, a daily death which could have but one ending, the death on Calvary when the body He had offered was bathed with His blood. Your offering, too, involves an immolation. I mean a day-by-day dying to yourself, a daily denial of your desires and your self-love. It means that God will strip from you—increasingly as the years go on—your very human loves, even the satisfactions that are sinless. That is the partial, day-after-day immolation which will one day be climaxed in the ultimate immolation, the most difficult death of all. For God will ask of you, as He asked of His Son, that you be "obedient unto death" (Phil 2:8).

Death, for anyone who loves God, is his final act of faith. It is the last affirmation of his belief in the tremendous truth which the Mass for the Dead declares each day: "For those who believe, life is not taken away; life is merely changed."

Death, for anyone who loves God, is his supreme act of confidence. At that unique moment, when you see so clearly how little worthy of any love you are, only a courage God-given will let you frame the final words that fell from Calvary: "Father, into thy hands I commend my spirit" (Lk 23:46). Few Christians can laugh at death, or even, with St. Paul, long for it. But every genuine Christian dies, like Paul, with high hope that death is, for him, a "gain" (Phil 1:21).

Above all, death is an act of love without parallel. If, as our Lord insisted, "greater love than this no man hath, that a man lay down his life for his friends" (Jn 15:13), then surely the most remarkable expression of love is to surrender my life simply because the God I love asks it. If you can do that—despite the pain, despite the tears—then you can echo the impassioned cry of Peter to his Lord: "Thou knowest all things: thou knowest that I love thee" (Jn 21:17).

35. In the Hand of God

IF THERE is bewilderment abroad about any facet of Catholic belief, there is bewilderment about purgatory. We are told that the whole idea is notorious nonsense, that Catholic purgatory is only a less harrowing form of hell, that even if there is such a thing, there isn't much we can do about it. This afternoon, therefore, let me ask three questions. First, is there such a thing as purgatory? Secondly, what is purgatory like? And finally, is there anything you and I can do about purgatory?

The first question, therefore: is there such a thing as purgatory? Be realistic. Some day—perhaps today, perhaps thirty years from today—you will die. 140,000 do each day. What will happen to you? This. Your soul will leave your body. That body will return to the earth from which it came. "Dust thou art, and unto dust thou shalt return" (Gn 3:19). But your soul, that part of you which cannot crumble into dust, will go to a judgment seat, a court, where the judge is God, you are on trial for your life, and the trial covers everything you thought and said and did during your hours on earth. What sentence will God pronounce on you?

If, at death's split-second, your face is frozen against God, if your soul is blackened by one serious sin not yet forgiven, then you will hear from the lips of Christ the most shocking words in the world: "Depart from me, cursed one, into the everlasting fire which was prepared for the devil and his angels" (Mt 25:41). But that is not purgatory; that is hell.

If, at the moment of death, no mortal sin blackens your soul, if the slightest offense against God has already been forgiven, if during life you have, by prayer and penance, by good works and suffering, paid the very last price that God exacts even after sin has been forgiven, then, pure as the mountain snows, your soul will hear from the lips of Christ the most beautiful words in the world: "Come, blessed of my Father, possess the kingdom prepared for you from the beginning of the world" (Mt 25:34). But that is not purgatory; that is heaven.

But suppose you are in neither of these two states. You cannot be imprisoned in hell, because your mortal sins have been forgiven. You cannot enter heaven, either because your soul is still stained by venial sin unrepented, or because you have not paid the full price exacted by God for sin. Only the spotlessly clean, only the perfectly pure, can enter heaven. So, then, you must be made pure; you must be cleansed from the spots that soil your soul and keep it from seeing God face to face. That is purgatory.

The second question: what is purgatory like? The one thing to cling to is this: purgatory is not a suburb of hell; it is the anteroom, the vestibule, of heaven. The paradox of purgatory lies in this: the soul is unbelievably sad and incredibly happy. The soul in purgatory is sad. You see, purgatory is punishment, because purgatory is purification. And because purgatory is punishment, there is pain in purgatory. And the most intense pain is gathered up in one simple fact: the soul hungers and thirsts for God, and God hides His face.

If you have ever tasted desire unsatisfied—if you have known the agony of love, where absence is anguish, and union alone can give peace—multiply that a thousand times and you will glimpse the anguish of a soul that is so near to God and yet so far. There is no merciful slumber, no distraction, no other interest: there is only God. And God hides His face. What other pain God uses to prepare your soul to enjoy Him days without end, we do not quite know. Whatever it is, it is as nothing compared to the burning yearning of a soul impatient, on fire with love unfulfilled.

And yet the souls in purgatory are incredibly happy. How can that be? There is, to begin with, a tremendous joy, a joy you and I can never have as long as we abide on earth, a joy that is possible only in purgatory: they know for certain that the day will dawn when they will see God face to face. They can never lose their Lord again, because they can never sin against God again. No matter what happens, God will come and take them to Himself. They know that, and in their knowledge is their joy. They are holy souls, saints, and, in the lovely words of Scripture, "the souls of the saints are in the hand of God" (Wis 3:1).

That joy no man can take from them. Our own earthbound love, even our love of God, is an anxious love. We cannot promise ourselves that it will be there tomorrow. The beauty of love on earth lies often in its blindness. The thrill of love in purgatory lies in its luminous certainty, the utter knowledge that on the threshold lies Love Divine. That is why I can make my own the insight of a saint, St. Catherine of Genoa: apart from the happiness of the saints in heaven, there is no joy comparable to the joy of the souls in purgatory.

More than that: the souls in purgatory *want* to suffer. That sounds strange, doesn't it? That anyone should want to suffer. But just think for a moment. Imagine a lovely young lady on the way to her birthday party. Her father and mother, her friends and relatives, all are waiting for her. She has put on an attractive white dress, spent a good deal of time on her hair, done everything a normal girl would do. On the way an accident occurs: her face and hands are scratched, her dress is spattered with mud. Now tell me, will that young lady pick herself up and, just as she is, sweep into the party? Won't she be glad of any chance to brush up, clean her dress, doctor her wounds, make herself presentable? That is how a soul in purgatory reacts. Somewhere along the way to God, somewhere on the road to its birthday in heaven, an accident occurred, perhaps a good many accidents. The soul was seared, the lovely white garment of its innocence was spotted. And the soul remembers now the words of the priest at baptism: "Receive this white garment and carry it without stain before the judgment seat of our Lord Jesus Christ, that thou mayest have eternal life." It knows it cannot see God the way it is; and so it does not want to. It knows it must suffer to doctor those wounds; and so it wants to. It is the age-old truth that Dante expressed in the *Divine Comedy*: "His will is our peace."[1] There you discover the sweet reasonableness of purgatory. Unending union with Purity itself, inconceivable intimacy with Holiness itself, demands perfect purity, holiness unhindered. The holy souls are glad to suffer, because suffering hastens the day of His coming.

A final question: what can you do about purgatory? There is a touching passage in the Second Book of Maccabees. Judas Maccabaeus and the men of his army are burying the bodies of their comrades who have met death fighting for freedom to worship God as their fathers had done. And they find that these heroes have disobeyed God: they are wearing on their lifeless breasts amulets that have been offered to idols. And God tells us through His Scripture: "And so they fell to prayer, pleading that the sin might go unremembered. Judas

---

1 Dante, *Divina Commedia: Paradiso*, Canto 3.

himself, their gallant commander, sent 12,000 silver pieces to Jerusalem, to have sacrifice made there for the guilt of their dead companions. Was not this well done and piously? Here was a man kept the resurrection ever in mind; he had done fondly and foolishly indeed, to pray for the dead, if these might rise no more, that once were fallen! And these had made a godly end; could he doubt, a rich recompense awaited them? A holy and wholesome thought it is to pray for the dead, for their guilt's undoing" (2 Mac 12:42–46).

"A holy and wholesome thought it is to pray for the dead." You, my friends, have within your hands an extraordinary power. These are prisoners, and you hold the key. You can take a soul in purgatory, perhaps a dear one departed, and lead that soul to God in heaven. Who knows? Your own turn may come. It will be consoling then to realize that there are saints in heaven pleading for you, for the saint in purgatory who once persuaded God to take them to Himself. It may well be your prayer that moves God to murmur to a soul departed the words a priest murmurs over a soul departing: "Let angels lead thee into paradise!"

36. Depart from Me

CATHOLIC THEOLOGY, the twentieth century insists, is a cruel theology. And that cruelty, which begins with man's conception in sin, finds its logical climax with man's cremation in hell. As a French philosopher has phrased it: "In the name of justice, a theology foreign to the spirit of mercy, foreign therefore to the spirit of Christianity, condemns to evils without end sinners who die without repentance—almost all of humanity." And the theologian Renan: "The dogma of eternal punishment contradicts what we know of God and His goodness; it is the palpable proof of the Church's inhumanity; it steals from the Church a token of truth."[1]

This evening, at the risk of appearing cruel, I should like to present the Christian case for hell. I shall do that in three stages: I shall tell you, first, *that* hell is; second, *what* hell is; and third, *why* hell is.

The fact of hell is rooted in a single powerful sentence: "When the Son of Man shall come in His majesty . . . He shall say to those on His left hand: 'Depart from me, cursed ones, into the everlasting fire which was prepared for the devil and his angels' " (Mt 25:31, 41). Now these are not the words of an Old Testament Jeremias threatening destruction

---

[1] These two texts are quoted by Jean Guitton in his chapter, "L'Enfer et la mentalité contemporaine," in the volume (by Michel Carrouges *et al.*) entitled *L'Enfer* (Paris: Editions de la Revue des jeunes, 1950), pp. 326, 328–29.

to God's enemies; this is not the thunder of a fiery-eyed Savonarola. These words fell from the lips of the gentlest of men. The Man who drew an adulteress from the dust when the pitiless would have stoned her. The Man who charmed children into His arms to bless them. The Man who wept over His doomed city, wept over His dead friend. The Man who caught more joy from one sorrowing sinner than from ninety-nine saints. The Man whose last breath from a cross was an act of love for every human being. The Man who was God.

So, then, hell is sober fact. The Church avows a hell because Christ her Lord avowed it. But concretely, what *are* the facts of hell? There are two which the Son of God stressed: "Depart from me . . . into everlasting fire." "Depart from me." The most significant, the least tolerable torture in hell is the anguish of loss. Man's purpose in life, his reason for living, is God; but in hell he has lost God, unalterably—and he knows it. His whole being cries out for its Creator, and its Creator is out of reach, eternally. There is no point in living; but live he must, unendingly. Fancifully, it is as if an eye knew it could never see; an ear, that it could never hear; a withered hand, that it could never touch.

This is essential frustration. Not just some individual, partial rebuff, temporary, tolerable. No, this is the one frustration that cannot be endured. For the substance of hell is separation, endless alienation, a gulf between man and the God for whom he was fashioned. Made for God, I am literally Godless. Made for love, I am literally loveless. Made for union, I am alone—forever.

"Into everlasting fire." There, in the language of a loving Lord, is the second of hell's unique agonies. It is a fire that is mysterious, a fire that is real, a fire that is endless. It is mysterious, of course; for how are we to conceive a fire that can touch an untouchable soul, a fire that can burn a body without corrupting it? But, for all its mystery, it must be real: not quite the flames that scorch our earth, but still an instrument of God that induces in the damned an acute anguish akin to the agony of the fire we know. And, on God's own word, it is a flame that will never be quenched.

But Catholic theology, while it refuses to belittle hell fire, refuses likewise to exaggerate it. For the fire of hell, intolerable as it is, is relatively unimportant. It is there, yes; but more important is what is *not* there: God. And in the absence of God, no other presence will gratify. For, in the absence of Life, what living thing will vivify? In the absence of Love, what creature will seem lovable? In the absence of Beauty, what lovely thing will thrill? In the absence of Joy, what is there to soften sorrow?

So then, hell *is*; and hell is the endless absence of God, the endless presence of fire. But why? Is this not to unmake a God whose very being is love, and to remake Him in our own image of hate? No. The point is: the twentieth century has lost its hold on hell because it has lost its sense of sin. Sin, you see, is not a matter of social taboo—what the "right people" don't do, at least in public. You will not grasp sin's essence save in terms of God's majesty. For sin—serious sin —is treason. It is the creature's rebellion against the Creator who framed him, the slave's revolt against the Master who owns him utterly. God commands, and man responds in the language of Lucifer: "I will not serve." Even more distressingly, God offers His love, and man rejects it. God dies for man, and man refuses to live for God. And this God is not just a friend whose friendship I am free to take or leave. In His friendship lies my happiness, in His love my hope. If I die His enemy, I have made my own hell. For if with my dying breath I am still determined to live without God, then I shall—for all eternity. Sin is separation from God; hell simply seals that separation forever. In one sense, then, hell is the logical climax of sin: severance from God here, severance from God hereafter. If it is true, as Scripture has it, that "The fool hath said in his heart: There is no God" (Ps 13:1), more foolish still is the human being who says "There is a God" and yet loses Him consciously, deliberately, in full possession of his senses.

More than that. In sin, man does not simply turn from God. He turns to a creature. He has made some creature, some thing, his god. It may be wealth, it may be power, it may be another human being, it may be his own intellect, his own lust, his own glory, his own hate. Whatever it is, he has set a creature on a pedestal and bent low in adoration. As St. Ignatius Loyola put it so simply: "the other things on the face of the earth were created for man's sake, to aid him in the prosecution of the end for which he was created"[2]—to help him serve God, to help him reach God. In sin, man overturns God's plan for human living: a creature becomes his god. And in hell, man pays for his misuse of creatures: a creature, fire, torments him, and no creature will give him joy. He is alone, with his pain and his memory of what might have been. Alone—save for angels turned devils; alone—save for men who have lost all reason for living, all reason for loving.

May I recommend for your meditation a prayer of Ignatius Loyola, a prayer that sums up the Catholic attitude to hell? I ask you, dear God, "for an interior sense of the pains which the lost suffer, in order that if I through my faults forget the love of the Eternal Lord, at least the fear of punishment may help me not to fall into sin."[3] If I forget love. . . .

2 *The Text of the Spiritual Exercises of Saint Ignatius* (4th ed. rev.; Westminster, Md.: Newman, 1943), p. 12.

3 *Ibid.*, pp. 26–27.

37. Come, Blessed of My Father

In Catholic thinking there is a strange paradox. For many of us, hell is a reality, heaven is not. Oh yes, we believe in both. We believe that the Son of God will not only thunder "Depart from me, cursed ones, into everlasting fire" (Mt 25:41); we believe He will murmur "Come, blessed of my Father, possess the kingdom prepared for you" (Mt 25:34). But "everlasting fire" provokes a picture; the picture is terrifying; and because I am terrified, I want no part of hell. But "the kingdom of heaven" is a colorless phrase; there is little for my imagination to feast on, little to attract me; and because I am not attracted, I am not sure I want any part of heaven. Heaven and hell both repel me, but for different reasons. Hell repels me because it frightens me; heaven repels me because it baffles and it bores me. The poet Francis Thompson captured the problem in eight strong lines entitled "Heaven and Hell":

"'Tis said there were no thought of hell,
    Save hell were taught; that there should be
A Heaven for all's self-credible.
    Not so the thing appears to me.
'Tis Heaven that lies beyond our sights,
    And hell too possible that proves;

[215]

For all can feel the God that smites,
But ah, how few the God that loves!"[1]

This morning I shall try to make heaven a little more meaningful to you. For the more you grasp its meaning, the more attractive will heaven grow.

My first affirmation is quite abstract, but it is awfully important. Heaven is fulfilment; for heaven is desire sated, heaven is happiness at its most perfect, joy undying. In this life there simply is no perfect fulfilment. There is always something I want and cannot have. Or I can have it, but it will mean an agony of achievement. Or, when I do achieve it, I cannot possess it as completely as I should like. Or I do possess it completely, but it grows bitter in my grasp; it palls, and I look for something else, for something more satisfying. And even if I am satisfied, there is still the realization that this is not forever; this will pass; this will grow old; this will die. I may be content, but I am not complete. It matters not where my happiness lies—in dollars beyond counting, in power beyond resisting, even in the many-splendored thing called love. Happiness in this world is like man in this world: it is a finite and a fleeting thing.

Not so heaven. What I am made for, that I shall have. Whatever I can want when in heaven, that shall be mine. Not for an uncertain moment, trembling like quicksilver in my grasp. No, fulfilment will be mine forever. Take the happiest hour you have ever lived, multiply it in intensity a thousand times, prolong it till time be no more—and you will have a faint suggestion of the happiness that is heaven.

All well and good; but what is this fulfilment in the concrete? What is it that will make me so devastatingly happy? The answer is at once a confession of profound ignorance and

---

1 Francis Thompson, "Heaven and Hell," ed. Wilfred Meynell, *op. cit.*, p. 219.

an assertion of thrilling truth. The confession of ignorance is the admission of St. Paul. Here was a man who "was caught up into paradise and heard secret words that man may not repeat" (2 Cor 12:4). And this man had to confess: "Eye has not seen nor ear heard, nor has it entered into the heart of man, what things God has prepared for those who love Him" (1 Cor 2:9). Of course heaven is mysterious, beyond human imagining. For the thrilling truth about heaven is this: heaven, at its simplest, is God.

Heaven is God. But not as we grasp God now. Here below, man's knowledge of God is a pale and bloodless thing. Here below, I have an *idea* of God: He is Supreme Being; He is infinite; He is unchangeable; He is everywhere; He is all-good; He knows all things. At times there is more. At times I spy Him in the gentle rain and I hear His voice in the thunderbolt; mortal man has touched Him in the flesh of Christ; my tongue has pillowed Him, and my heart has been His home; my mind is glutted with His revelation. But even then I must confess with the prophet Isaias: "Indeed thou art a hidden God" (Is 45:15).

Not so in heaven. John the Evangelist summed it up when he wrote: "we shall see Him just as He is" (1 Jn 3:2). Just as He is. Father, Son, and Holy Spirit: three Persons, one God; I shall see Him just as He is. Not with my eyes of flesh, the way I look lovingly on my mother or gaze in fascination on a star. It is my mind that will possess Him—not a picture of God, not an idea of God, but God Himself. My mind will come into immediate contact with the living God—nothing between us, not even an idea. We have never had this kind of knowledge; the closest thing to it is the way I know myself; but even that is a far cry from the vision that is heaven. I shall know God somewhat as God knows Himself.

And my knowledge of God will have but one rival, one

equal: and that is my love. For this contact between God and man is a contact between persons, not airy, unsubstantial shapes. In heaven we have not a cold meeting of minds but a warm, intimate friendship. This is union at its most perfect, this is love at its loftiest. Here at last man must, and God can, give in total abandon.

Heaven, then, is God: God within us in incredible knowledge, in breathless love. That is why we can make our own the poetic insight which a perceptive nun has shared with us under the title "Discovery":

> "It's this that makes
> My spirit spin,
> My bones to quake,
> My blood run thin,
> My flesh to melt
> Inside my skin,
> My very pulse
> Create a din—
> It's this that makes
> My spirit spin:
> That Heaven is
> Not *up*, but *in!*"[2]

Stranger still, the ecstasy of that first moment of knowledge, the rapture of that first moment of love, will never dull. Do you recall the legend of Michelangelo's Moses? They tell us that when Michelangelo gave the final stroke to his Moses, he stepped back from the statue; he looked, and he was transfixed in rapture. So alive was it, so vital, that he hurled his hammer at his creation and cried: "Speak!" Take that moment, make it endless, transform the lifeless Moses into the

[2] Sister Mary Ignatius, "Discovery," in *Messenger of the Sacred Heart* 77, no. 2 (Feb., 1942), 58.

living God—and you may begin to suspect what we mean by eternal ecstasy, unceasing delight.

There is much else in heaven. I shall see, transfigured far beyond Thabor, the flesh of the lovable Lord who lived and died for me: the smile on His lips, the wound in His side; but, unlike Peter, James, and John, I shall not be afraid. I shall find a gracious Lady, and like Elizabeth of old I shall whisper in wonder: "How have I deserved that the mother of my Lord should come to me?" (Lk 1:43). I shall live unendingly with apostles like Andrew, with confessors like Columban, with martyrs like Thomas More, with intellectuals like Augustine and humble priests like the Curé of Ars; yes, with angels like Gabriel. I shall love my dear ones as Christ our Lord loves His mother. But it will always remain true that heaven is, above all, God: "through Him and with Him and in Him" I shall give of my heart to all others.

To me it is significant that those men and women have yearned most for heaven who have loved most, who have tasted God's love for them and burn with love in return. Take St. Ignatius of Antioch. It is about the year 110. Ignatius is in chains, on the road to Rome, to death by wild beasts in the Colosseum. And he begs the Christians of Rome not to use their influence with the state, not to show him what he calls "unseasonable kindness." No, he writes:

"Suffer me to be the food of wild beasts, which are the means of my making my way to God. God's wheat I am, and by the teeth of wild beasts I am to be ground, that I may prove Christ's pure bread. . . . I would rather die and come to Jesus Christ than be king over the entire earth. Him I seek who died for us; Him I love who rose again because of us. . . . Do not make a gift to the world of one who wants to be God's. . . . My Love has been crucified, and I am not on fire with the love of earthly things. But there is in me a 'Living

Water' which is eloquent and within me says: 'Come to the Father.' "[3]

My dear friends: A saintly bishop, centuries ago, used to caution his people: don't worry where hell is, but how to stay out of it! May I offer a similar gem of advice about heaven? Don't worry how God can possibly keep you happy in heaven; make it your concern to get there!

[3] Ignatius of Antioch, *Letter to the Romans* 4, 1; 6, 1; 7, 2; translated by James A. Kleist, S.J., in *Ancient Christian Writers* 1 (Westminster, Md.: Newman, 1946), 81–83.

A NOTE ON THE TYPE

IN WHICH THIS BOOK WAS SET

This book has been set in Weiss, an interesting face created by E. R. Weiss of Germany, who prefers to be called a painter. While he has studied almost every known letter in the world and copied inscriptions from Roman monuments, Renaissance capitals and fantastic baroque letter-forms from gravestones, he still remains a painter. The Weiss types, while traditional letters, are the product of our own time. Lines of text take on a gracious air—an easy, limpid flow when set in this modern type design. Weiss types have good color and create dignity whenever one sees them, either in a book or advertisement. This book was composed and printed by the York Composition Company, Inc., of York and bound by Moore and Company of Baltimore. The design and typography are by Howard N. King.